AF470576

FRANCIS FRITH'S

MELTON MOWBRAY TOWN AND CITY MEMORIES

*For Bob on Fathers Day, 20th June
2010,*

All our Love,

Jackie, Wendy, Steve and Harley

THE FRANCIS FRITH COLLECTION

www.francisfrith.com

MELTON MOWBRAY

SARAH STIRLING and JULIA ELLIS both read English at nearby
Leicester University and share a keen interest in local history.
Sarah has lived in the area all her life. Her family home is in Waltham
on the Wolds, a picturesque village just a few miles north of Melton
Mowbray. A keen horse-rider, Sarah has explored many of the scenic
bridlepaths found around Melton Mowbray and in the Vale of Belvoir.
Julia prefers walking to riding, but is equally passionate about
Leicestershire and its rich history. Both Sarah and Julia share two other
local interests - porkpies and Stilton cheese.

The Baptist Church c1955 M60043

FRANCIS FRITH'S
TOWN & **CITY**
MEMORIES

MELTON MOWBRAY

SARAH STIRLING AND JULIA ELLIS

First published as Melton Mowbray, A Photographic History of your Town
in 2001 by Black Horse Books, an imprint of The Francis Frith Collection®
Revised paperback edition published in the United Kingdom in 2005 by
The Francis Frith Collection as Melton Mowbray, Town and City Memories

Limited hardback edition 2005
ISBN 1-84589-049-3

Paperback edition 2005
ISBN 1-85937-975-3

Text and Design copyright © The Francis Frith Collection®
Photographs copyright © The Francis Frith Collection®
except where indicated

The Frith® photographs and the Frith® logo are reproduced under licence from
Heritage Photographic Resources Ltd, the owners of the Frith® archive and trademarks.
'The Francis Frith Collection', 'Francis Frith' and 'Frith' are registered trademarks of Heritage Photographic Resources Ltd.

All rights reserved. No photograph in this publication may be sold to a third party other
than in the original form of this publication, or framed for sale to a third party.
No parts of this publication may be reproduced, stored in a retrieval system, or transmitted,
in any form, or by any means, electronic, mechanical, photocopying, recording or otherwise, without the prior permission of
the publishers and copyright holder

British Library Cataloguing in Publication Data

Melton Mowbray
Town and City Memories
Sarah Stirling and Julia Ellis

The Francis Frith Collection®
Frith's Barn, Teffont,
Salisbury, Wiltshire SP3 5QP
Tel: +44 (0) 1722 716 376
Email: info@francisfrith.co.uk
www.francisfrith.co.uk

Aerial photographs reproduced under licence from Simmons Aerofilms Limited
Historical Ordnance Survey maps reproduced under licence from Homecheck.co.uk

Printed and bound in England

Front Cover: **MELTON MOWBRAY, SHERRARD STREET c1955** M60036t

The colour-tinting in this image is for illustrative purposes only,
and is not intended to be historically accurate

Every attempt has been made to contact copyright holders of illustrative material.
We will be happy to give full acknowledgement in future editions for any items not credited. Any information
should be directed to The Francis Frith Collection.

FRANCIS FRITH'S
TOWN & CITY
MEMORIES

CONTENTS

F rancis Frith, Victorian founder of the world-famous photographic archive, was a devout Quaker and a highly successful Victorian businessman. By 1860 he was already a multi-millionaire, having established and sold a wholesale grocery business in Liverpool. He had also made a series of pioneering photographic journeys to the Nile region. The images he returned with were the talk of London. An eminent modern historian has likened their impact on the population of the time to that on our own generation of the first photographs taken on the surface of the moon.

Frith had a passion for landscape, and was as equally inspired by the countryside of Britain as he was by the desert regions of the Nile. He resolved to set out on a new career and to use his skills with a camera. He established a business in Reigate as a specialist publisher of topographical photographs.

Frith lived in an era of immense and sometimes violent change. For the poor in the early part of Victoria's reign work was a drudge and the hours long, and ordinary people had precious little free time. Most had not travelled far beyond the boundaries of their own town or village. Mass tourism was in its infancy during the 1860s, but during the next decade the railway network and the establishment of Bank Holidays and half-Saturdays gradually made it possible for the working man and his family to enjoy holidays and to see a little more of the world. With characteristic business acumen, Francis Frith foresaw that these new tourists would enjoy having souvenirs to commemorate their days out. He began selling photo-souvenirs of seaside resorts and beauty spots, which the Victorian public pasted into treasured family albums.

Frith's aim was to photograph every town and village in Britain. For the next thirty years he travelled the country by train and by pony and trap, producing fine photographs of seaside resorts and beauty spots that were keenly bought by millions of Victorians.

The Rise of Frith & Co

Each photograph was taken with tourism in mind, the small team of Frith photographers concentrating on busy shopping streets, beaches, seafronts, picturesque lanes and villages. They also photographed buildings: the Victorian and Edwardian eras were times of huge building activity, and town halls, libraries, post offices, schools and technical colleges were springing up all over the country. They were invariably celebrated by a proud Victorian public, and photo souvenirs – visual records – published by F Frith & Co were sold in their hundreds of thousands. In addition, many new commercial buildings such as hotels, inns and pubs were photographed, often because their owners specifically commissioned Frith postcards or prints of them for re-sale or for publicity purposes.

In order to gain some understanding of the scale of Frith's business one only has to look at the catalogue issued by Frith & Co in 1886: it runs to some 670 pages. By 1890 Frith had created the greatest specialist photographic publishing company in the world, with over 2,000 stockists! The picture on the right shows the Frith & Co display board on the wall of the stockist at Ingleton in the Yorkshire Dales (left of window). Beautifully constructed with a mahogany frame and gilt inserts, it displayed a dozen scenes.

POSTCARD BONANZA

The ever-popular holiday postcard we know today took many years to appear, and F Frith & Co was in the vanguard of its development. Postcards became a hugely popular means of communication and sold in their millions. Frith's company took full advantage of this boom and soon became the major publisher of photographic view postcards.

Francis Frith died in 1898 at his villa in Cannes, his great project still growing. His sons Eustace and Cyril continued their father's monumental task, expanding the number of views offered to the public and recording more and more places in Britain, as the coasts and countryside were opened up to mass travel. The archive Frith created continued in business for another seventy years. By 1970 it contained over a third of a million pictures of 7,000 cities, towns and villages. The massive photographic record Frith has left to us stands as a living monument to a special and very remarkable man.

This book shows your town as it was photographed by this world-famous archive at various periods in its development over the past 150 years. Every photograph was taken for a specific commercial purpose, which explains why the selection may not show every aspect of the town landscape. However, the photographs, compiled from one of the world's most celebrated archives, provide an important and absorbing record of your town.

THE EARLY TOWN

RIGHT: THE RIVER EYE 1927 80307

RIGHT: THE RIVER EYE 1927 80307

BELOW RIGHT: BELVOIR CASTLE c1965 M60188

The beautiful Vale of Belvoir lies to the north and west of Melton with Belvoir Castle dominating the northern escarpment. It is Leicestershire's most important stately home and the most interesting historical site in the area.

BELOW: ST MARY'S CHURCH 1927 80310

The parish church of St Mary the Virgin was built in the 13th and 14th centuries at a time when Melton Mowbray prospered from the wool trade. It is the size of a small cathedral and is considered the most magnificent church in Leicestershire.

THE EARLY TOWN

On the banks of the River Eye in North Leicestershire (80307, left) stands Melton Mowbray, an historic market town renowned for its rural tradition and its famous pork pie. The town is surrounded by ancient villages such as Burton Lazars, Freeby, Sysonby, Welby and Eye Kettleby, and it is generally agreed that 'Melton' is derived from its position as 'middle town'.

In 1875 a local farmer discovered 50 skeletons buried in neat rows in his field. The remains were surrounded by beads, knives, shields, spearheads, buckles, an extraordinarily long sword and several urns. This pagan Anglo-Saxon burial ground, the first of several found in the area, testifies that Melton was a settlement as long ago as the 6th century. By the time of Edward the Confessor Melton was a small community ruled by the lord of the manor, Lewric Fitz Lewin. A description of the town at this time can be found in the Rev J Ward's 'Melton Mowbray in Olden Times', 1879. He writes: 'there were several mills in the vicinity which were worked by the neighbouring streams, and also a good-sized wood, measuring about a furlong square'.

According to the Domesday Survey, by 1086 'Medel Tune' was a thriving market town with a population of 270 inhabitants, two water mills, two priests and a Norman overlord named Goisfrid de Wirce. Following the death of de Wirce, the Melton estate was divided between Nigel de Albini and Robert de Mowbray (originally Montbrai), Earl of Northumberland. In 1096 de Mowbray joined a revolt against the despised King William Rufus and was thrown into prison. His estates passed to Nigel de Albini, whose son Roger, assumed the name of Mowbray, by order of Henry I. According to Ward: 'for noble rank and high estate, for martial bravery and renown, they [the de Mowbrays] had few if any equals'.

Melton was occupied by Parliamentarian forces during the Civil War. In 1645 a battle took place at nearby Ankle Hill. Sir Marmaduke Langdale, commanding a Royalist force of 1,500 men, inflicted severe losses on the Roundheads. Following his return to power, Charles II knighted Sir Henry Hudson, who was the lord of the manor in Melton and a fervent Royalist. The occasion was marked by a feast in Sherrard Street, which lasted several days and involved the roasting of a whole ox outside the Limes.

During the 18th century most Meltonians lived within easy walking distance of the church and the Market Place. The roads were

THE EARLY TOWN

GENERAL VIEW C1955 M60086

THE EARLY TOWN

in a terrible condition and consequently the town lacked commercial industry. In 1790 a much-needed canal was built joining Melton Mowbray to the Leicester to Loughborough Navigation and things began to look up for the town.

The 19th century saw the improvement of Melton Mowbray's roads and the arrival of Melton railway station, with connections to Peterborough and from there, to London. New technology made farming much faster and easier. As a result, the town grew and prospered. At the same time the upper classes rediscovered hunting as an elegant and exciting pastime. Melton stood in prime hunting territory and rapidly became the sport's centre. For this reason the industrial revolution of the 19th century largely passed the town by. The surrounding area, which encompasses the lush Vale of Belvoir with its famous castle (M60188, pages 8-9) remains to this day full of grassland, gated roads and picturesque buildings constructed from local ironstone.

THE APPROACH TO THE TOWN CENTRE 1932 85176

Burton Road Bridge and the parish church can be seen in the distance.

THE CATTLE MARKET C1955 M60042

Melton Mowbray's central position has long assured the success of its market. Not only is the town surrounded by a great many local villages and hamlets but it is also on the route of the ancient drove roads from the north, such as the A1 and the Fosse Way. Melton market is the only one in Leicestershire significant enough to be recorded by the Domesday Survey of 1086, by which time it was well established. Local legend has it that the market received a Royal Charter from Edward the Confessor in the days when Leofric ruled Mercia with his wife, the famous Lady Godiva, and when Lewric Fitz Lewin was Lord of the Manor at Melton.

Two ancient annual fairs, held in Whit Week and the Feast Day of St Lawrence are thought to be almost as historic as the market. From the mid 19th century to the beginning of the First World War, three new annual fairs were added. According to Brabner's Gazetteer of 1895 the fairs were 'chiefly for horses, cattle, and sheep, though the fair in Whitsun-Week is also largely for pleasure'. The Stilton Cheese Fair was the most famous. It took place in the Market Place where traders built towers of Stilton cheese on beds of straw.

Throughout the 18th and 19th centuries the hunting boom, combined with better roads and a railway station, caused Melton to grow and prosper and both the cattle and sheep markets flourished. The Town Estate purchased and then demolished a row of buildings in the Market Place to provide more room for expansion. Despite this measure, the market filled the Market Place and stretched from the bottom of Sherrard Street to the Half Moon in Nottingham Street, and from the church in Burton Street to the George in the High Street. The sheep market extended the whole length of one side

THE MARKET

THE SHEEP MARKET c1955 M60027

The market also deals in cattle and pigs. Notice the Melton Farmers Association
Office to the left of the scales.

of Nottingham Street, selling about 50,000 sheep annually. Sherrard Street the site of the cattle market and originally known as the Beast Market was equally congested on market day with some local shops forced to close as pens filled the street. When the pens were cleared away both streets remained filthy with mud, straw and manure. Clearly something needed to be done. In 1870 the Town Wardens and Feoffees leased land between Scalford and Nottingham roads from the Town Estate and built a new cattle, sheep and pig market.

At this time Lord Melbourne was the lord of the manor. He owned the rights to the market, as well as a great deal of property in the town centre and a large expanse of land to the north and west of the town, including the Play Close, where many of the fairs were held. The market and fairs had become a time-consuming concern for Lord Melbourne. Following the Play Close Riots in the late 19th century, he agreed to sell the Play Close and the rights to the market to the Town Estate.

The Old White Swan figurine above W H Pearce Outfitters (85169, page 16) has interesting history. The expression 'to paint the town red' originated in Melton Mowbray. In 1837 the Marquis of Waterford was joined by a party of friends for the Croxton Park races. The group ran riot for several nights, running rings around the local constabulary and antagonising the local population with their exploits. They broke the toll gates, wrenched off door knockers, threw the Red Lion sign into the canal and smeared everything in sight with red paint. The Marquis of Waterford personally painted the Old White Swan red as a grand finale.

For many years a large block of shops stood in the Market Place opposite F Warner (85169 and M60078, page 20, now Thomas Cook). W Barnes & Co (M60015, page 18) was the largest shop in 'Barnes Block'. It combined a general and fancy draper's, a milliner's, a dress and mantle maker's, gentlemen's mercers and funeral furnishers. Barnes Block was demolished in 1963 and the Market Place and adjoining streets were both expanded and pedestrianised.

Four ancient crosses once marked the different market sites: the Sheep Cross on Nottingham Street outside the King's Head; the Corn Cross at the junction of Nottingham Street and High Street; the Sage Cross on the junction of Sherrard Street and Sage Cross Street; and the Butter Cross in the Market Place. As the markets expanded and moved to new sites the crosses were removed and sold. The Butter Cross, which had also served as the town's High Cross (158 marriages took place there after the Civil War) was replaced in 1986 to commemorate the 900th anniversary of the Domesday Survey. The platform is built from stones found in St Mary's churchyard believed to be the remains of an original cross. A new Corn Cross was erected 10 years later.

The Swan Inn (85169, page 16 and M60183, page 22) once covered a vast area, incorporating extensive stabling and outbuildings. In Tudor times it was the most important building after the church. It was the main inn, the venue for important business meetings, the town jail, and the town's armour was kept in the kitchen. In Georgian and Regency times local balls and assemblies were held here. Sad to say, the Swan Inn closed in 1825 and was converted into shops but the Old White Swan figurine can be seen above Dollond & Aitcheson today.

Compare M60183 below to 85169: modern signs now fill the middle distance and many locally-owned businesses have lost out. Curry's, for instance, is the new neighbour of the Melton Farmers Association. Notice the sign in the centre of M60183, which reads 'Diversion: Petfoods'. Chappie Ltd, a pet food factory, started business in 1951. Its large workforce caused a huge population increase and provided much prosperity for the town.

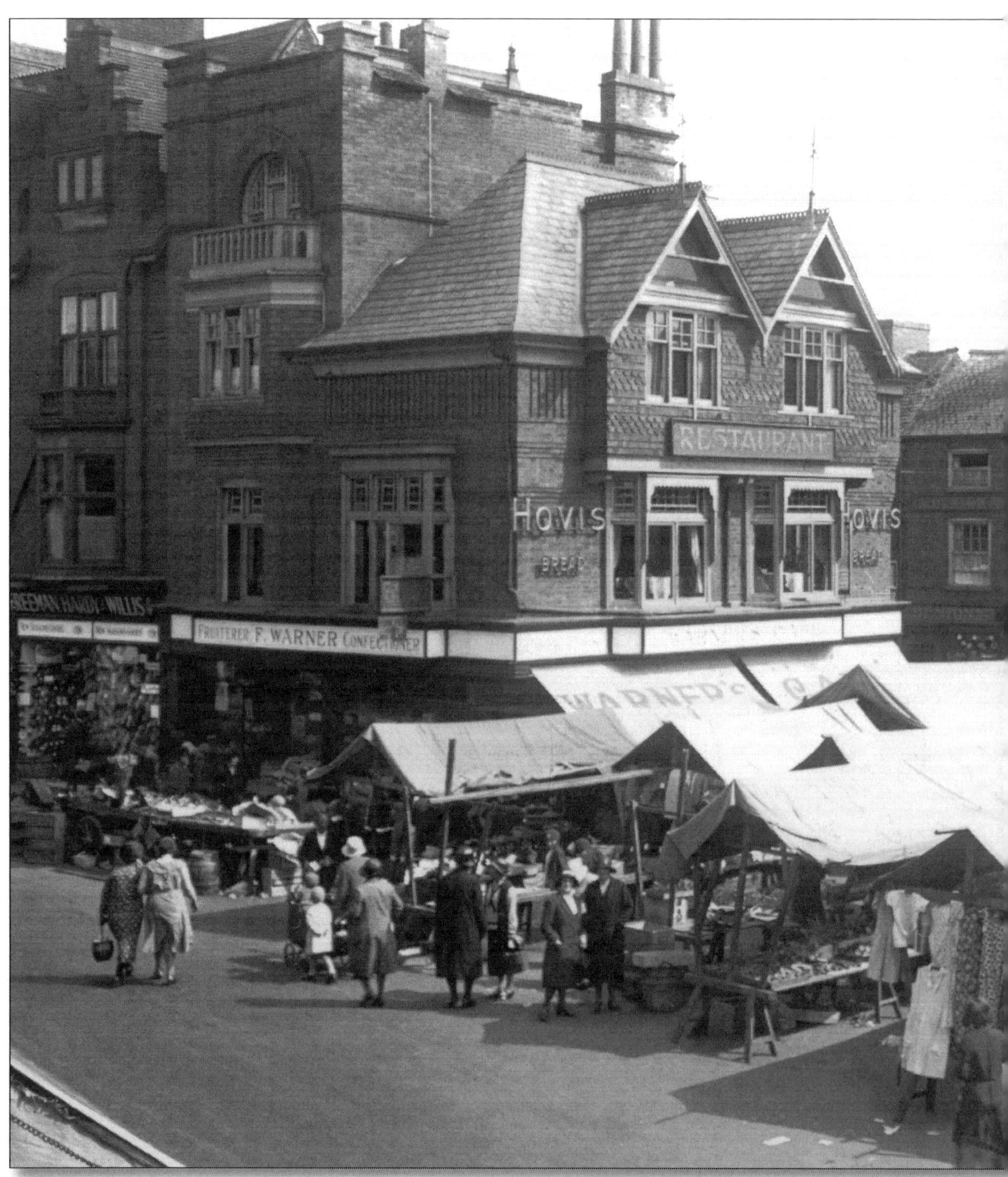

RESTAURANT
HOVIS
BREAD
HOVIS
BREAD
FRUITERER F. WARNER CONFECTIONER
FREEMAN HARDY WILLS

THE MARKET PLACE 1932 85169

The large market extends beyond the photograph in both directions. The Melton Farmer's Association Butchers Department (now Toolchest) was a neighbour of the Swan (Pearce's, right) for a long period: 'English Meat Purveyors' proudly adorns its façade. The building is also visible in M60183, page 22.

THE MARKET

BELOW:
THE MARKET PLACE C1960 M60105

Looking towards the Market Place from the junction of Burton Road. Barnes Block is in the centre. Notice the new street light outside Melia's (centre right).

BELOW RIGHT: Detail of M60105

THE TOWN ESTATE

The Town Estate is a charitable organisation that has been of great benefit to Melton Mowbray for hundreds of years. It was established in the 16th century, at the time of the Reformation. Henry VIII wished to reclaim the extensive areas of land that had belonged to the Catholic church and to religious institutions such as the monasteries. The rents and revenues from Melton's church lands had been used to provide many services, including paying the schoolmaster. Meltonians were unsurprisingly reluctant to part with these benefits, and some of the lands were hidden from the Royal Commissioners, and secured for use by the townspeople. The lands were then looked after by a number of Feoffees, or Trustees, on behalf of the Town Estate, and the income continued to benefit the whole community.

In the past the Town Estate provided Melton with a wide range of services, from free schools to street lighting. Today, the charity's main functions are running the street markets and providing numerous parks and leisure facilities for the town. The Town Estate recently celebrated its 450th anniversary and continues to thrive. The fact that this ancient institution has survived into the 21st century is truly unique.

THE MARKET

RESTAURANT
LUNCHEON
TEA
Cafe
PORK
PIES
NER CONFECTIONER
PORK PIES
WARNER'S CAFE
TONS

THE MARKET

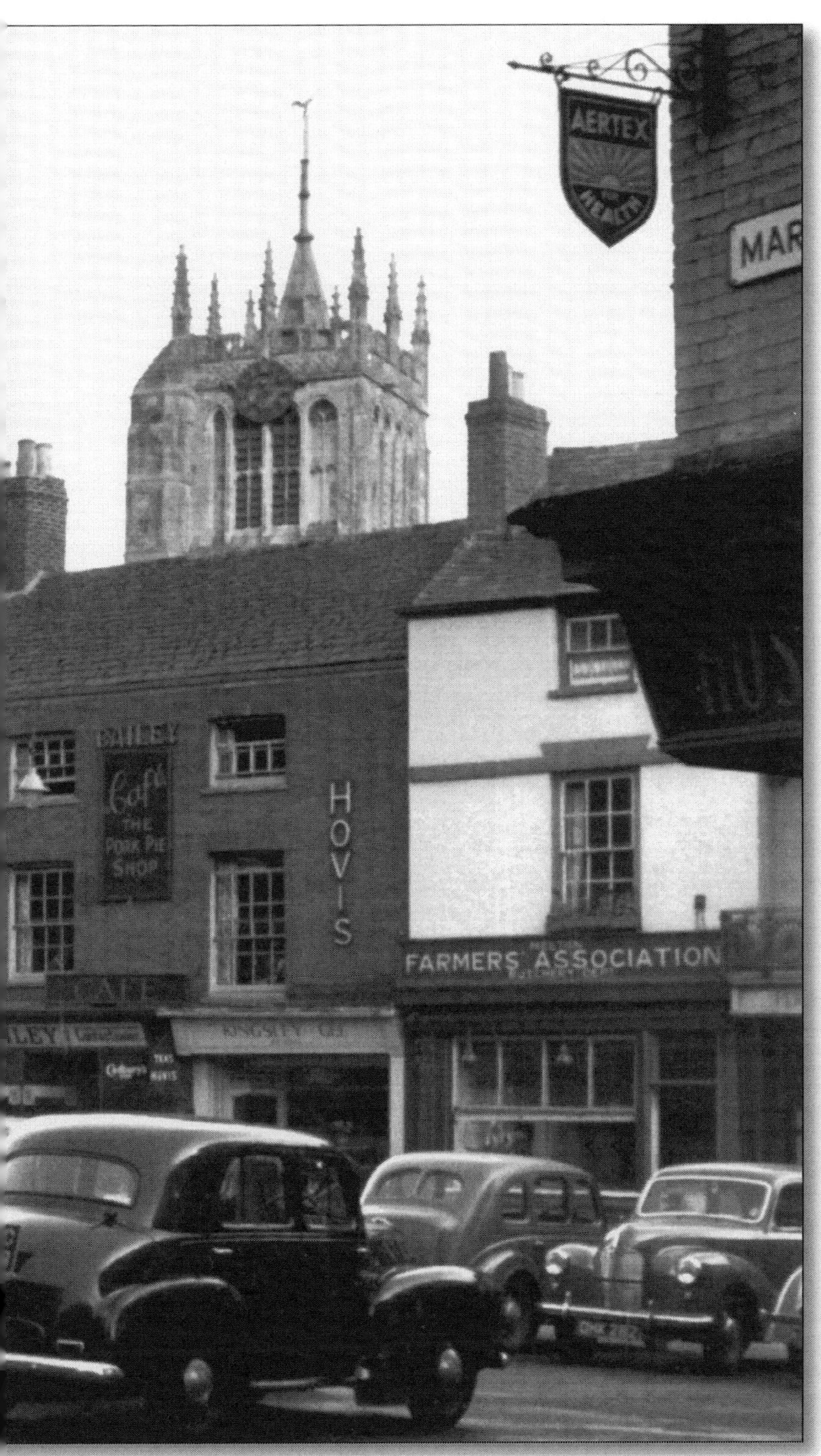

THE MARKET PLACE c1955
M60078

Besides W Barnes, F Warner was the other
large shop in the Market Place.
It combined a fruiterer, a confectioner,
a pork pie shop, a restaurant and a café
serving luncheon and tea. Mr Warner also
found time to run a catering business.

THE MARKET PLACE c1965 M60183

The pedestrians on the far left are outside WH Smith & Sons. An 8ft stone wall at the back of this shop and a stone foundation in the cellar which reaches ten feet below the pavement, are medieval. It is very likely that this was the site of the original de Mowbray manor. A huge ancient fireplace found in the Three Tuns on King Street may also have been part of the property.

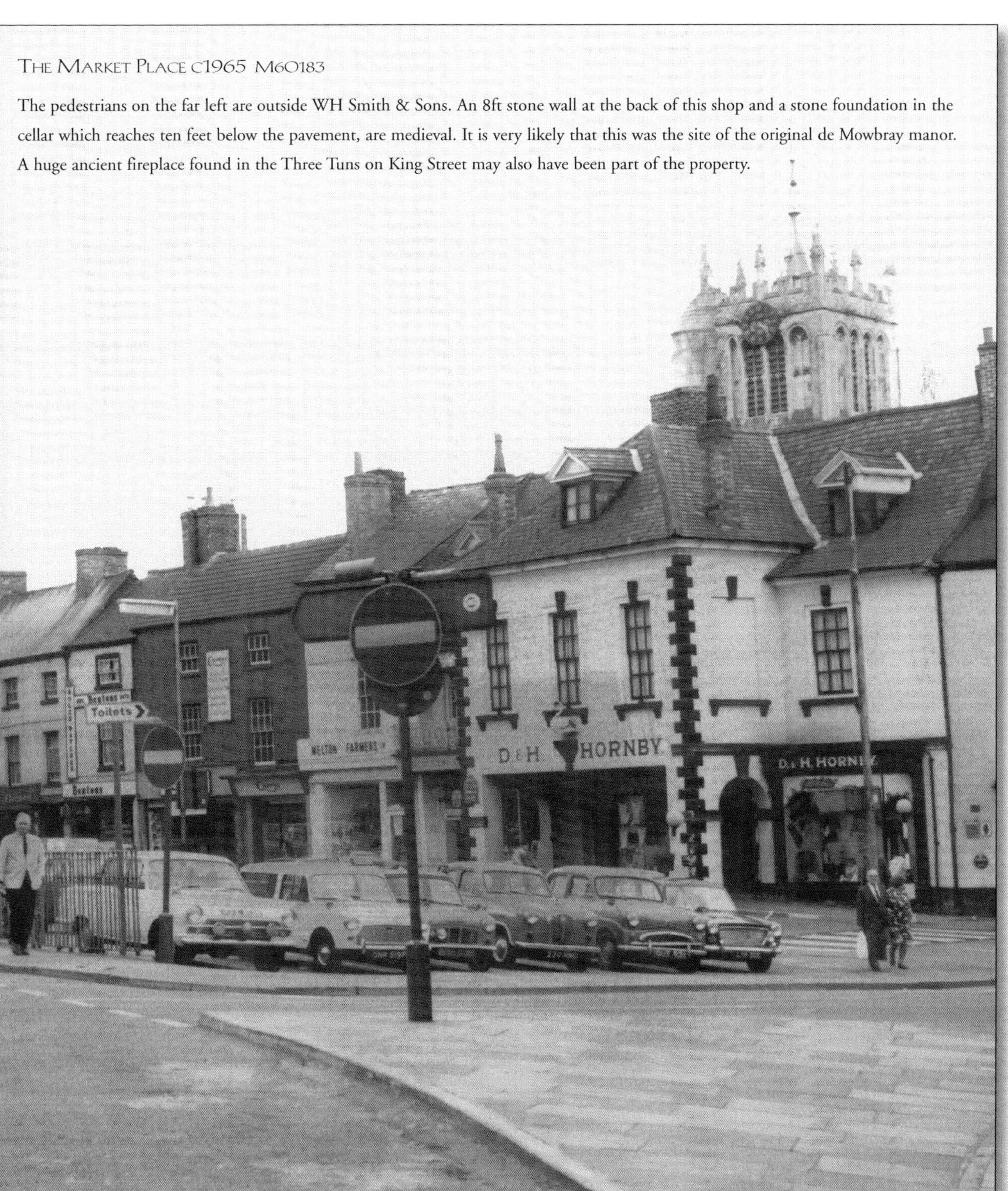

LOCAL DELICACIES

Today the town is most widely known for the world-famous Melton Mowbray pork pie, which originated in Melton in 1831. Edward Adcock, who ran a bakery adjacent to the Fox Inn in Leicester Street, recognised the popularity of his cold meat pies among visiting fox hunters. Adcock decided to market his pies in London, which proved to be a huge success. By 1840 the increased demand allowed Enoch Evans to set up a rival business in the Beast Market, which is now Sherrard Street, and the popularity of the Melton Mowbray pork pie began to grow. These hand-raised pies are uniquely rounded, made from the finest British uncured pork and encased in rich and crunchy pastry. Dickinson and Morris, who run Ye Olde Pork Pie Shoppe in Nottingham Street, are the last remaining firm in Melton to bake the authentic pies on their shop premises. The bakery was founded in 1851 and has since become a huge tourist attraction, with as many as 250,000 visitors each year.

Dickinson and Morris, along with many other shops in the town, also sell another of Melton's famous delicacies Stilton cheese. Stilton was first developed in the villages to the east of Melton Mowbray, possibly as early as the 14th century. The cheese became famous when Mrs Frances Pawlett, a dairywoman who lived near Melton Mowbray, entered into a business arrangement with Cooper Thornhill, who agreed to market her cheese. Thornhill was the owner of the Bell Inn at Stilton in Cambridgeshire, which acted as a staging post for people travelling along what is now the A1 between London and York. He began to introduce the cheese to travellers staying at the inn, and its popularity spread rapidly. The cheese then took its name from the town, despite the fact that it has never actually been made in Stilton.

Stilton, a creamy, blue-veined cheese, has become known as 'The King of Cheeses'. Today a 16lb Stilton cheese takes 17 gallons of milk to produce and at least two months to mature. Stilton is one of the few cheeses to have been granted a 'protected designation of origin' status by the European Commission. This means that there are strict codes for the quality of the cheese, and it can only be made in the counties of Leicestershire, Derbyshire or Nottinghamshire. Only seven dairies are licensed to produce Stilton, one of which is Tuxford and Tebbutt in Melton Mowbray.

It is no coincidence that Melton's two most renowned delicacies originated in the same region. Pigs thrive on whey, which is the chief by-product of cheese making, and so Stilton and pork pies were made side by side. Tuxford and Tebbutt, who make speciality cheeses on their premises in Thorpe End, are an example of the amalgamation of the two industries. The company was formed when a pie shop, which opened in 1867, joined forces with a local cheese

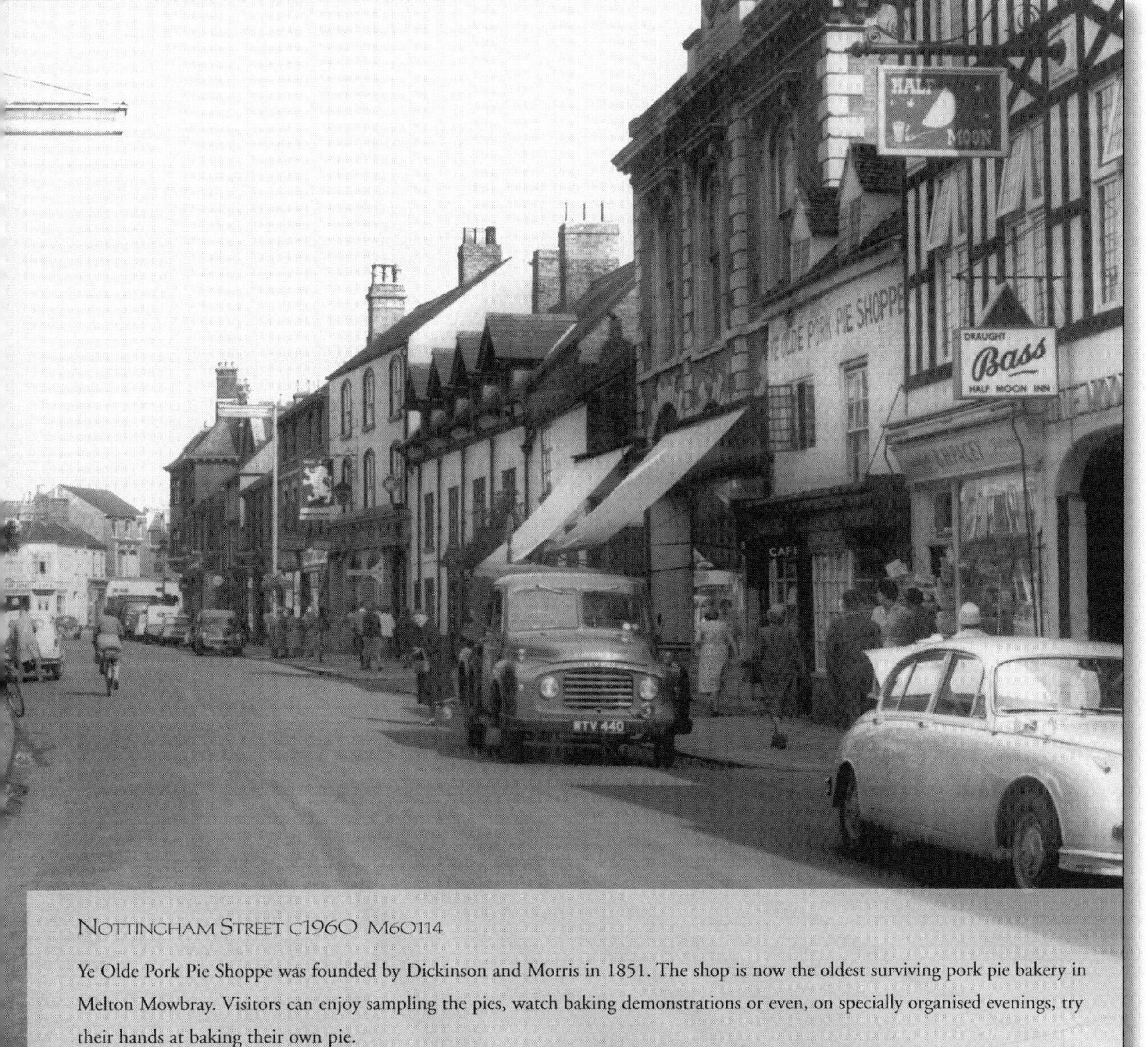

NOTTINGHAM STREET C1960 M60114

Ye Olde Pork Pie Shoppe was founded by Dickinson and Morris in 1851. The shop is now the oldest surviving pork pie bakery in Melton Mowbray. Visitors can enjoy sampling the pies, watch baking demonstrations or even, on specially organised evenings, try their hands at baking their own pie.

makers. The company still thrives today, but it is now solely devoted to cheese making.

Since 1954, Dickinson and Morris has also been the exclusive producer of the Melton Hunt Cake. This cake is made using a mixture of dried fruit, with a generous helping of old Jamaican rum. Like the pork pies, Hunt Cake was greatly enjoyed by the visiting hunting community, who carried these delicious refreshments in their saddlebags.

Melton Mowbray has a history of providing visitors with culinary delights. Many shops selling these local specialities still exist today, and visitors can even take part in a Pork Pie and Stilton Cheese trail, visiting shops around the streets of Melton Mowbray.

HUNTING

The hunt passes through Scalford.

Throughout the winters of the 18th and 19th centuries, the small town of Melton Mowbray was a temporary home for marquises, royal dukes, financiers and wealthy industrialists. Even the Prince of Wales and the occasional Hungarian count joined the throng. The town was almost as popular as London with Europe's richest families and as many fortunes were squandered here as in the capital. The reason? Hunting had boomed, and Melton Mowbray, lying within easy reach of all the premier Shire packs, became its Mecca.

A large number of hunting lodges and boxes were built in the town for the huntsmen, their staff and their horses. Brabner's Gazetteer of Britain (1895) states that 'extensive stables capable of holding 1000 horses' for 'leading sportsmen from all parts of the kingdom' had been erected by 1895. Egerton Lodge, home of the Earl and Countess of Wilton, was the most fashionable place in Melton Mowbray at this time. The 2nd Earl of Wilton was dubbed 'King of Melton'. Cantering through the town, behaving badly at one of the inns or clubs on fashionable Burton Street the hunting set chased foxes six days a week, and caused a great

deal of mayhem both day and night. In the 1880s one gentleman made a bet that he could ride his horse up and down the stairs. Unfortunately, he managed to fulfil only half of this wager and his horse lived in the upstairs drawing room until it was removed through the window by a hoist.

In the preceding century, the village of Quorn, home of the most widely-known hunt in Great Britain, had been the most fashionable place to be seen in hunting circles. Mr Hugo Meynell entertained many parties of nobility and gentry at his home, Quorndon Hall. However, neighbouring Melton Mowbray soon became more popular. The town's very insignificance proved its attraction. Its abundance of gated roads, green lanes, wide verges and cut and laid hedgerows made it the perfect hunting ground.

The Quorn hunt was founded in 1696 by Mr Thomas Boothby. It covers a vast 'country' stretching roughly from a few miles south of Nottingham in the north to the Leicester City boundary in the south. In 1853 Sir Richard Sutton was Master of the Quorn. He felt that its country was too large and so he delegated the area of south Leicestershire known as 'Billesdon country' to his son, Richard. This became known as the Fernie Hunt.

The Cottesmore hunt is based in Rutland and Leicestershire, bordering with the Quorn on the west side. It can trace its origins back to 1666, when Henry, Viscount Lowther brought a pack of foxhounds to the East Midlands from Lowther Castle in Westmorland. The Lowther family retained a connection with the pack for 250 years. The famous Lord Lonsdale, known as the 'Yellow Earl', was Master of the Cottesmore in the early 1900s. The Belvoir Hunt dates from 1750. Until 1896 the Dukes of Rutland generally held the Mastership.

The Belvoir country lies in Leicestershire and Lincolnshire, extending from Melton Mowbray and Newark in the west to the North Sea in the east.

Throughout the 21st century, hunting faces ever-increasing opposition, with very passionate views on either side of the debate. After years of wrangling, a ban was forced through the courts in 2005. The last legal hunt took place on February 18th 2005.

BURTON STREET

Anne of Cleves House 1927 80300

Burton Street has changed a great deal since these early times. Notice the horseback rider and the dogs in the street, there was very little traffic. The 14th-century Anne of Cleves House is the low, unostentatious building at the end of the row, in front of the church.

Anne of Cleves House was originally a chantry for the priests of Melton Priory. It later became the parsonage house and is still sometimes referred to as the Old Rectory. In 1583 Henry VIII gave the house to his favourite, Thomas Cromwell. A few years later, when Cromwell fell from favour and was beheaded, the house was reclaimed. It was then given to Anne of Cleves as part of her divorce settlement. However, there is no record of her ever visiting the house.

The Bede House, a famous almshouse, was built and endowed by Robert Hudson in 1640. It stands opposite Anne of Cleves House (M60017, page 28 and M60081, pages 32-33). Six poor men lived here and were provided with coal, food, money and a sermon from the vicar every Plough Tuesday. The building is a shelter for senior citizens today. The front windows were originally stained glass, featuring Henry Hudson's coat of arms. The building was considerably renovated in 1891 and the glass was moved to the window in the south aisle of the nave of St Mary's church, nearby.

A great many 19th-century aristocrats rented purpose built 'hunting boxes' on fashionable Burton Street for the hunting season. Many of these houses, 'boxes' only in comparison to the stately homes of their owners, are still in evidence today. Majestic porches, bay windows, archways that once led through to stables; Burton Street is full of architectural relics from Melton Mowbray's days as 'Queen of the Shires.' The acclaimed Christopher Stavely is responsible for much of the new building work carried out at this time. He is known to have used materials from several ancient buildings, including the old de Mowbray manor house in King Street, to build hunting boxes in the town.

The Old Club House (M60005, page 30) had room for only four tenants but still managed to throw huge dinner parties several nights a week. Many famous huntsmen, including the Prince Regent, the Duke of York, the famous Berkley Craven and Beau Brummel,

BURTON STREET

RIGHT:
ANNE OF CLEVES HOUSE C1955 M60034

Compare this to 80300, page 27. The house has now been transformed into a popular café. The thick-walled, stone-built and buttressed structure helped preserve the Anne of Cleves House: it is the oldest building in Melton Mowbray apart from the church.

BELOW:
THE BEDE HOUSE C1950 M60017

Taken from the Almshouse's private gardens.

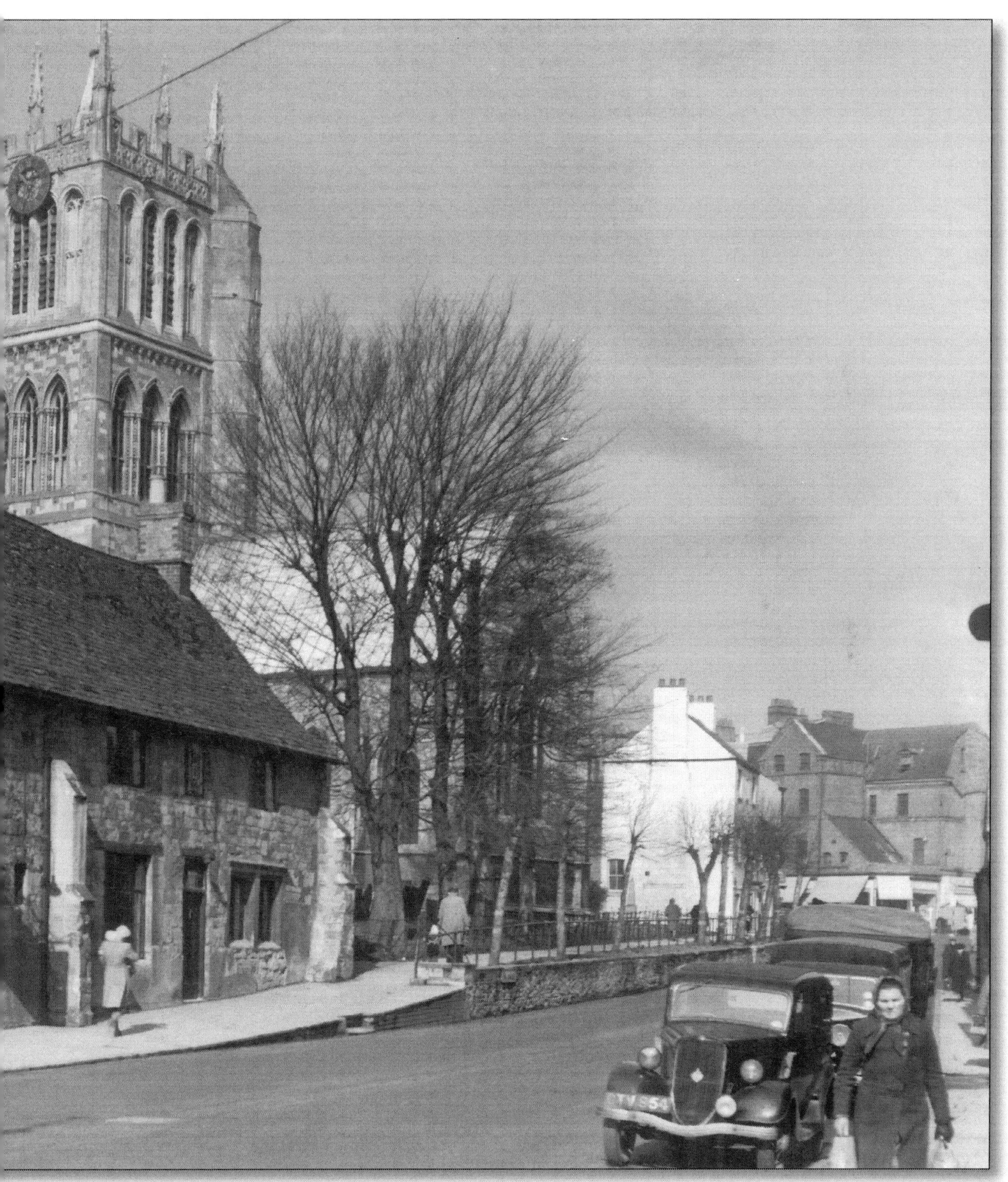

BURTON STREET

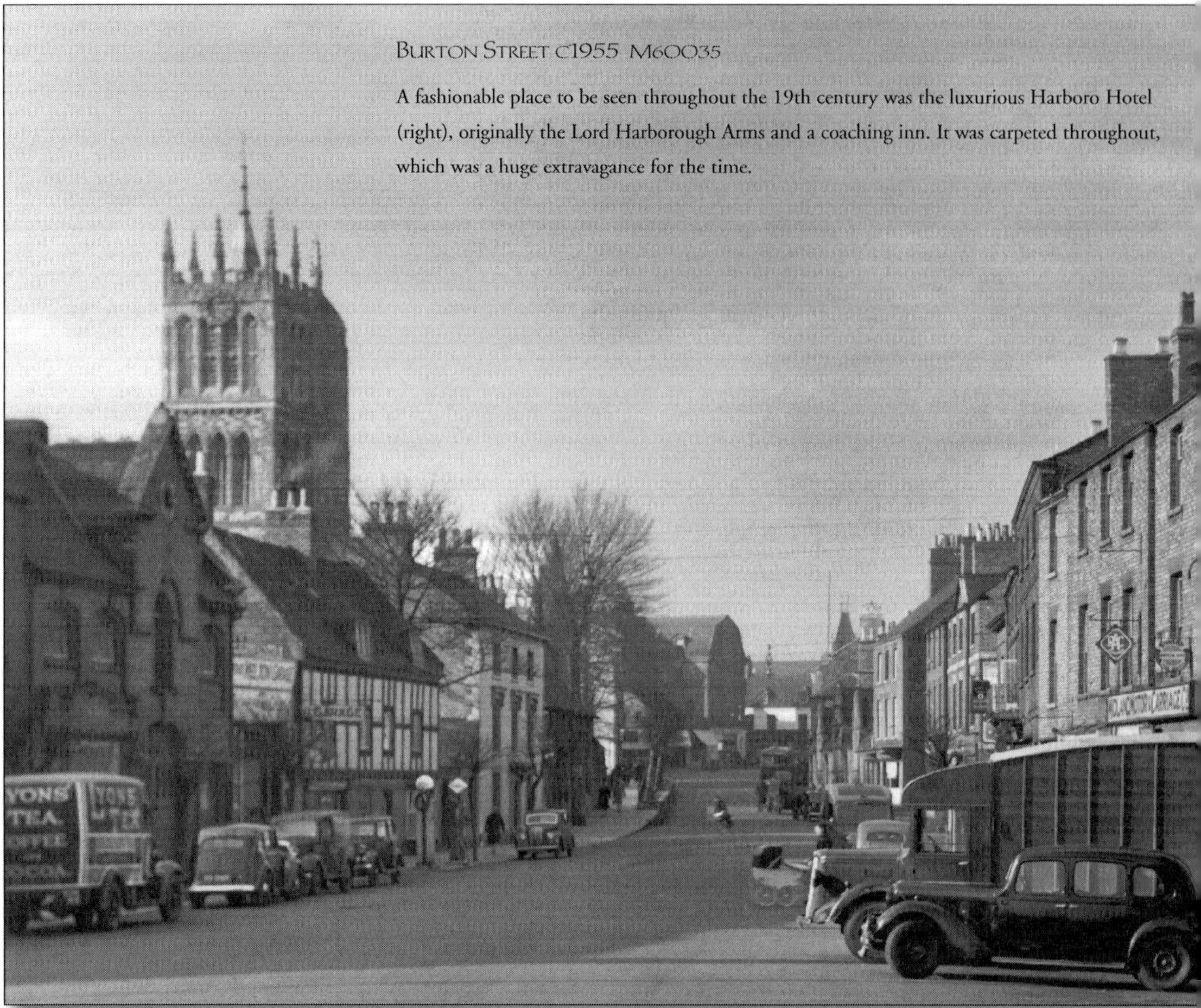

BURTON STREET c1955 M60035

A fashionable place to be seen throughout the 19th century was the luxurious Harboro Hotel (right), originally the Lord Harborough Arms and a coaching inn. It was carpeted throughout, which was a huge extravagance for the time.

BURTON STREET c1950 M60005

The Old Club House, which was the haunt of Melton Club from 1810 to the 1850s, stands on the far right. The upper storey of the Old Club remains relatively unchanged. Before the premises were transformed into a shop, a matching set of round bay windows graced the ground floor, and a porch stood between them.

frequented the Old Club. Major General the Hon Berkley Craven, known as the 'Gambling Dandy', shot himself after incurring insurmountable debts. Beau Brummel, dubbed 'King of the Dandies', was England's eccentric leader in the world of fashion.

The building next to the Old Club, but hidden from sight, is the Blakeney Institute, formerly the Vicarage. The Colles Hall was built next to it in 1870, on the site of the old George and Dragon. It is a memorial to Dr Colles, once the vicar of Melton, who implemented a great deal of structural renovation in the church. Together with the celebrated architect, Gilbert Scott, Colles saved the finest church in Leicestershire from collapse.

Coventry House at the end of Burton Street was one of the town's first hunting boxes. Sir Harry Goodricke, 7th baronet of Ribston and Master of the Quorn, lived here in the 1830s. Sir Harry was popular for his generosity and respected for his hunting skills. On the day of his funeral local businesses in the town closed for the day. Shortly afterwards, Coventry House became a fashionable club founded by Edward Montague, 5th Baron Rokeby.

Brabner's Gazetteer describes Melton as possessing 'several large and high-class hotels, which are patronised during the season by hunting men', and the Harboro Hotel was doubtless one of them. The Dukes of Devonshire, Sutherland, Portland, Beaufort and Somerset spent seasons here, and so did many earls and a large number of foreign princes, noblemen, and even the Maharajah of Cooch Behar. Her Royal Highness the Empress Elizabeth of Austria, reputedly the most beautiful woman in Europe, signed the guest book in 1874 and hunted with the Belvoir. Her cortège of noblemen and horses filled the hotel and stables to overflowing.

Cardigan House is one of the most elegant buildings on Burton Street. It has changed little (externally, at least) since it served as the home of the famous Brudenells, the last Earl and Countess of Cardigan. The Earl, renowned for leading the disastrous charge of the Light Brigade, died in 1868 from a hunting accident. The eccentric Countess continued to live in the house, and was often seen in her old age sitting on the balcony wearing extravagant make-up and a huge curly wig.

The Red Lion once stood next to Cardigan House with its malt house attached. This pub had the distinction of being the last thatched building in Melton Mowbray. It lost its licence in 1928 and was demolished two years later.

BURTON STREET

Burton Street and the Bede House c1955   M60081

BURTON STREET

BURTON STREET

Plans for a Midland railway station in Burton End were announced in 1845. The railway faced much opposition, both from the local population and the hunting set. It was feared that the countryside and the hunting ground would be spoiled by an ugly scar of rail track. The 6th Earl of Harborough proved the most formidable opponent. This was not surprising, as the plans originally showed the railway passing through the grounds of his home, Stapleford Park. Surveyors were repeatedly chased away by the Earl's gamekeepers in the famous 'Battle of Stapleford'. Eventually a compromise was reached, and the station opened in 1847. Melton Mowbray was now connected to London by rail and a new era had begun.

BURTON STREET C1965 M60144

Compare this photograph to 80300 on page 27. The Morris Service Depot and the church are the only clues that the two photographs feature the same street.

SHERRARD STREET

This photograph shows the view along Sherrard Street towards Thorpe End. On the left is Woolworth's, which is still there today. Woolworth's and the neighbouring businesses occupy the former site of the gardens of one of Melton's most prized historical buildings: The Limes.

This photograph was taken from the opposite direction, looking towards the Market Place.

SHERRARD STREET

S herrard Street was originally the home of Melton Mowbray's Beast Market. In 1870 the market was moved out of the town centre to the site of the present cattle market on Scalford Road. The street was called the Beast Market until the 1790s. The name was then changed to honour the Earl of Harborough from nearby Stapleford Hall, whose family name was Sherrard. The Earl was very generous to the people of Melton Mowbray, and in 1793 he paid for street lighting in the town. The town was lit using oil lamps, a privilege few other market towns of the time could enjoy.

During building work in the street in the 1950s, some ancient foundations were unearthed. It is thought that they belonged to a small religious house, possibly a priory of the Cluniac order. At the corner of Sherrard Street and Sage Cross Street is the site of the former Sage Cross. This was the trading post for herbs and spices, and it was the fourth and final one of the town's crosses to disappear. The cross is thought to have subsided beneath the road surface at the end of the 19th century.

Sherrard Street was once full of inns and taverns, such as the Old Bishop Blaize, which accommodated the many buyers and sellers who travelled from far and wide to visit the Beast Market. Today the street is largely made up of shops and commercial services.

Sherrard Street has unfortunately lost many of its finest old buildings. Woolworths now stands on the site of the former gardens of The Limes which was sadly demolished in 1932. The Limes was a an impressive Jacobean manor house, which had extensive grounds reaching to Kings Street in the north and Sage Cross Street in the east. It was originally home to Robert Hudson, one of Melton's greatest benefactors and the founder of the Bede Houses. The Limes was later home to the Stokes family, who were solicitors and also benefactors to the town. They lived in the house until the 1870s. All that remains of this fine house is the Bread Door, a wooden door with a hatch, through which bread was given to the poor in times of plague or famine. The door now stands in the wall of the memorial gardens at Egerton Lodge.

MELTON MOWBRAY FROM THE AIR 1962   AFA103785

NOTTINGHAM STREET

Nottingham Street is one of the oldest streets in Melton Mowbray. It was originally called Spital End (an abbreviation of Hospital End), after the Knights Hospitaller of the Order of the Hospital of St John of Jerusalem, who owned a chapel and a manor house on the east side of the street. This powerful military and charitable order was endorsed by the first Roger de Mowbray, Lord of Melton in the 12th century. He probably paid for the building of their property, which stretched roughly from the north end of the street to the White Lion Hotel. A reconstructed medieval wall believed to be part of the Hospitallers' property stands behind the White Lion.

In the early 20th century the Corn Exchange (M60075, far left) contained a large hall, a men's room, a club room, a library and the Magistrates' Court. It also provided the setting for a wide diversity of social events such as meetings, markets, dances and theatricals. By the 1980s Melton Mowbray had purpose-built magistrates' courts, a town library and a cinema. Formal balls and dances had also become much less popular. Since there seemed little use for the Corn Exchange beyond the venue for Town Estate meetings, the building was transformed into the Bell Shopping Arcade, which retains the original 19th-century façade.

Most of the property on the west side of Nottingham Street belonged to the Town Estate, with the notable exception of Latham

NOTTINGHAM STREET
c1955 M60075

On the far left is the Corn Exchange, built in 1855 by a board of local landowners and farmers. The Town Estate bought the building in 1919.

House. This was built in 1750 on land belonging to Sir Richard Raynes' trustees. Before his death in 1732, Sir Richard set up a trust for poor boys attending the free school. The rent of Latham House funded the clothing and education of six boys, each chosen for three years. The boys wore a distinctive bright blue and red uniform topped off with a jaunty tam-o'shanter, and a silver badge engraved with 'The Donation of Sir Richard Raynes'. This custom ended in the early 1900s.

The King's Head Hotel at the end of Nottingham Street (M60123, page 42) was established in the reign of Queen Victoria, but it has been extensively modernised. As late as the last century, the façade was inscribed with the advertisement 'Boxes for Hunters'.

The archway leading through to the beer garden, with its imposing black gates, is a relic of the hotel's days as a coaching inn.

The sheep market took up a large part of the street every Tuesday until 1870, when the cattle market was built on Scalford Road. It produced a great deal of trade for the street's public houses. In former times the street supported at least two others: the Green Dragon and the Eight Bells.

The various inns, hostelries and alehouses on Nottingham Street proved a popular meeting place for local organisations and societies in the 19th century. The Fire Brigade met at the Eight Bells when a fire alarm was raised, and the trustees of the Melton to Grantham turnpike met at the White Lion Hotel to discuss

41

NOTTINGHAM STREET

RIGHT:
NOTTINGHAM STREET C1955 M60031

This view looks from the junction of the High Street and South Parade on market day. The sign of the popular White Lion Hotel is just visible in the centre of this photograph and Barclays Bank (now Ladbrokes) is on the far left.

BELOW LEFT:
PARK ROAD C1960 M60123

BELOW RIGHT:
NOTTINGHAM STREET C1965 M60159

Melton Mowbray Building Society stands on the far right. Formed in 1875, it attracted two hundred shareholders within its first three months and has thrived ever since.

road-related problems. They may well have encountered the Society for the Prosecution of Felons, who also met regularly at the hotel. At this time Melton also boasted several Oddfellows Societies and Friendly Societies, as well as a Temperance Society and a Licensed Victuallers' Association.

Dickinson and Morris (Ye Olde Pork Pie Shoppe, M60114, page 44-45) is probably the most famous shop in Melton Mowbray. This pork pie and sausage shop has stood in Nottingham Street for the last 150 years, but the business existed long before this date. It outgrew its premises in Burton End and moved to the present site in 1851.

View M60159 (below) was taken about five years after M60114 and shows a much more contemporary scene: notice the road markings, and the double-decker bus outside the Bell Hotel in the distance. However, the old petrol pump built into the pavement outside Margaret Murray is a reminder that much more change is yet to come.

Nottingham Street's popularity caused congestion, so in 1928 the Urban District Council pulled down the 18th-century part of Egerton Lodge and built a car park and a relief road. Wilton Road now runs parallel to Nottingham Street, and joins Nottingham Road.

The shopkeepers and publicans along Nottingham Street, who feared loss of trade, did not support the building of this road. They need not have worried; now pedestrianised, Nottingham Street remains as popular as ever.

LEICESTER
PERMANENT
BUILDING SOCIETY

NOTTINGHAM STREET c1960 M60114

Notice the new street light and the new signs marking the White Lion Hotel, the Half Moon, and the Leicester Permanent Building Society (now the Alliance and Leicester).

South Parade c1955 M60077

SOUTH PARADE AND THE HIGH STREET

At the top of the High Street, Nottingham Street leads into South Parade. South Parade, and the neighbouring street, Cheapside (M60076, page 48), then join the Market Place. South Parade and Cheapside used to be separated by Barnes Block, which was demolished in 1963. Today there is only one road, one side of which is named South Parade, and the other Cheapside. The shops in the foreground on the right of M60077 form one side of Barnes Block. The Market Place is behind it to the right.

This area used to be called Cornhill, because it was the site of the original Corn Cross and the Corn Wall. The Corn Cross disappeared towards the end of the 18th century and the last recorded use of the Corn Wall was in 1814. The building of the Corn Exchange in 1854 meant that this site, where corn had been sold for hundreds of years was no longer needed. A replica Corn Cross was erected at this junction in 1996, and in the same year Queen Elizabeth II visited the town. At the replica cross she was presented with gifts of Melton Mowbray pork pie, Stilton cheese and Melton Hunt Cake.

The Bell Hotel, situated at the end of the High Street (M60076, page 48 and M60117, page 51) was known for many years as the Bell and Swan. Towards the end of the 19th century it became very popular among the hunting community. Today the Bell Hotel has been converted into a small shopping arcade. Note the shuttered sash windows of Boots the Chemist next door (M60117), which are typical of the Georgian period.

SOUTH PARADE AND THE HIGH STREET

CHEAPSIDE C1955
M60076

Cheapside was formerly called Butcher's Row. This photograph was taken from the junction of the High Street and Nottingham Street. Barnes Block is the group of buildings in the centre of the photograph and St Mary's church tower can be seen behind them. The road that continues round to the left, past the Bell Hotel and Boots the chemist, is South Parade.

SOUTH PARADE AND THE HIGH STREET

MAIN PICTURE: HIGH STREET C1960 M60112

RIGHT: HIGH STREET C1955 M60073

The High Street was, and still is, home to a number of banks and building societies. Lloyds Bank has now moved, and the building has been taken over by the Halifax. The Midland Bank (now called HSBC) and the neighbouring building, which is still the solicitors' firm Latham and Co, were originally the New Club.

FAR RIGHT: SOUTH PARADE C1960 M60117

SOUTH PARADE AND THE HIGH STREET

Photograph M60112 was taken from in front of the Bell Hotel, looking towards Egerton Lodge, which can be seen at the end of the street. On the right-hand side of the street is the George Hotel, the town's oldest surviving coaching inn. The George and many of the surrounding buildings were built in the 17th century. Formerly called the George and Talbot, it was once Melton's chief posting house, providing a change of horses and a resting point for travellers. In the hotel foyer the words 'Licensed to let post horses' are still painted on one of the beams. In the 19th century, when the railways led to the demise of coach travel, the George became a base for the hunting community. The hotel hosted hunt dinners for the visiting aristocracy, as well as attracting foreign sportsmen and visiting army officers.

The New Club (M60073, centre) was a spacious house built by the architect Staveley in the 1830s. Young aristocrats used the club as a base when they were staying in Melton during the hunting season. The New Club closed around 1840 when the building was taken over by the Leicestershire Banking Society.

COUNTY MAP

DERBYS
NOT
From Burton upon Trent
From Burton
DERBY
The Woulds
Blackfordby
Over Seal
Nether Seal
Part of DERBY
From Tamworth
WARWICK
Railway
Staunton Harrold
Worthington
Newbold
Cole Orton
ASHBY DE LA ZOUCH
Swannington
In Derby
Packington
In Derby
Measham
Normanton le Heath
Sweepston
Appleby
Snarestone
Norton
Shackerstone
Bilstone
Twycross
Orton on the Hill
Sheepy Magna
Sheepy Parva
Sibson
Newton
Odestone
Barton in the Beans
Congerston
Carlton
Ashby de la
Temple Hall
Willsborough
Shenton
Upton
Ratcliffe Culey
ATHERSTONE
Witherley
Atterton
Fenny Drayton
Lindley
From Tamworth
Soar R.
From Coleshill
Hemington
Lockington
Castle Donnington
KEGWORTH
Diseworth
Isley Walton
Long Whatton
Breedon
Langley Priory
Belton
Hathern
Diskley
Thorpage
Sheepshead
Knight Thorpe
Garendon
LOUGHBOROUGH
Canal
Osgarthorpe
Gracedieu
Thringstone
Whitwick
CHARNWOOD
Wood Thorpe
Quorn
Beau Manor
Charley
Woodhouse
FOREST
Ravenston
In Derby
Snibston
Bardon Hill
Ulvercroft
Swithland
Hugglescote
Donnington
Normanton le Heath
Stanton under Bardon
Crapston
Heather
Ibstock
Markfield
Newtown Linford
Bagworth Pa
Horsepool
Anstey
Bagworth
Thornton
Grooby
Beau
Nailstone
Ratby
Anst
Barleston
Botcheston
Kirkby Frith
Glenfield
Newton
Kirkby Muxloe
LEIC
Osbaston
MARKET BOSWORTH
Newbold Verdon
Desford
Brascote
Cadeby
Peckleton
Lubbesthorpe
Sutton Cheney
Kirkby Mallory
Togley
Basset Ho.
Enderby
Thurlaston
Stapleton
Normanton Turville
Narborough
Dadlington
Earl Shilton
Huncote
Whetstone
Stoke Golding
Barwell
Elmsthorpe
Little Thorpe
Croft
Cosby
Higham on the Hill
Wykin
Stoney Stanton
Sutton in the Elms
HENCKLEY
Prime Thorp
Burbage
Sapcote
Sketchley
Aston Flamville
Broughton Astley
NUNEATON
Shanford
Dunton Bassett
Frowlesworth
Leire

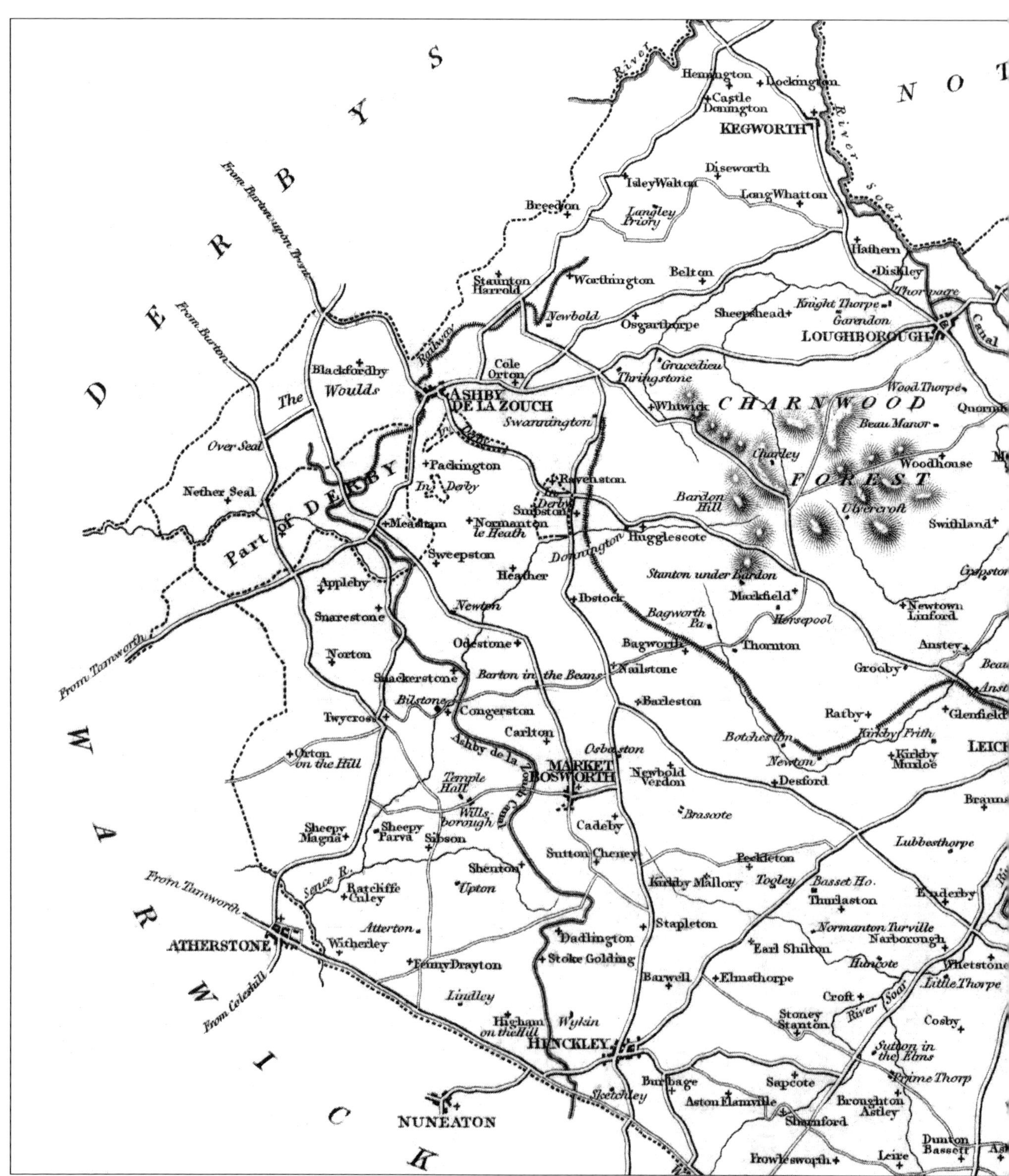

COUNTY MAP

N
SHIRE
RUTLANDSHIRE
VALE
From Nottingham
Road
Foss
The
Fosse
River Wreak
Leic. Canal
Union Canal
Oakham Canal
Hose
Eastwell
Eaton
Croxton Keyrial
Branston
Long Clawson
Goadby Marwood
Bescaby
Saltby
Nether Broughton
Waltham on the Woulds
Stonesby
Sproxton
Dalby on the Woulds
Scalford
Caldwell
Buckminster
neswould
Wartnaby
Holwell
Coston
uld
Abkettleby
Sewstern
ton on Woulds
Grimston
Welby
Garthorpe
Walton on the Woulds
Sax or Segs Hill
Saxelby
Freeby
Saxby
on Soar
Seagrave
Hoby
Shoby
Ragdale
MELTON MOWBRAY
Sysonby
Thorpe Arnold
Wyfordby
Wymondham
Ashfordby
Kirby Bellar
Eye Kettleby
Kirmond
Stapleford
Edmondthorpe
Thrussington
Frisby on the Wreak
Burton Lazars
Rotherby
Brooksby
Sileby
Kearsby
Great Dalby
Lit. Dalby
Leesthorpe
Ratcliff on the Wreak
Cossington
Syston
Gaddesby
Ashby Folville
Thorpe Satchville
Pickwell
Cold Overton
OAKHAM
Queenborough
Barsby
Burrow on the Hill
Somerby
North & Sth. Thurmaston
Barkby
South Croxton
Twyford
Newbold
Knossington
Barkby Thorpe
Beeby
Baggrave
Maresfield
Belgrave
Humberton
Lowesby
Newton Cold
Ouston
Whatborough
Humberstone
Keyham
Quenby
Halstead
Withcote
Scraptoft
Ingarsby
Tilton on the Hill
Bushby
Thurnby
Houghton on the Hill
Evington
Stoughton
Billesdon
Skeffington
Loddington
Knighton
Frisby
Gaulby
Tugby
UPPINGHAM
Oadby
Stretton Magna
Stretton Parva
King's Norton
Rolleston
East Norton
Allexton
Wigston Magna
Keythorpe
Histon on the Hill
Nosley
Goadby
Stockerston
Glen Magna
Barton Overy
Carlton Curlieu
Shangton
Hallaton
Horninghold
Holyoaks
Newton Harcourt
Wistow
Glooston
Cranoe
Blaston
Kilby
Stonton Wyville
Shawston
Holt
Peatling Magna
Kibworth Harcourt
Turlangton
Medbourne
Great Easton
Arnesby
Fleckney
Kibworth Beauchamp
Church Langton
W. & E. Langton
Thorpe Langton
Welham
Drayton
Bringhurst
ROCKINGHAM
Smeeton Westerby
Saddington
Shearsby
Gumley
ntingthorpe
River Welland

LEICESTERSHIRE COUNTY MAP SHOWING MELTON MOWBRAY AND SURROUNDING AREAS c1850

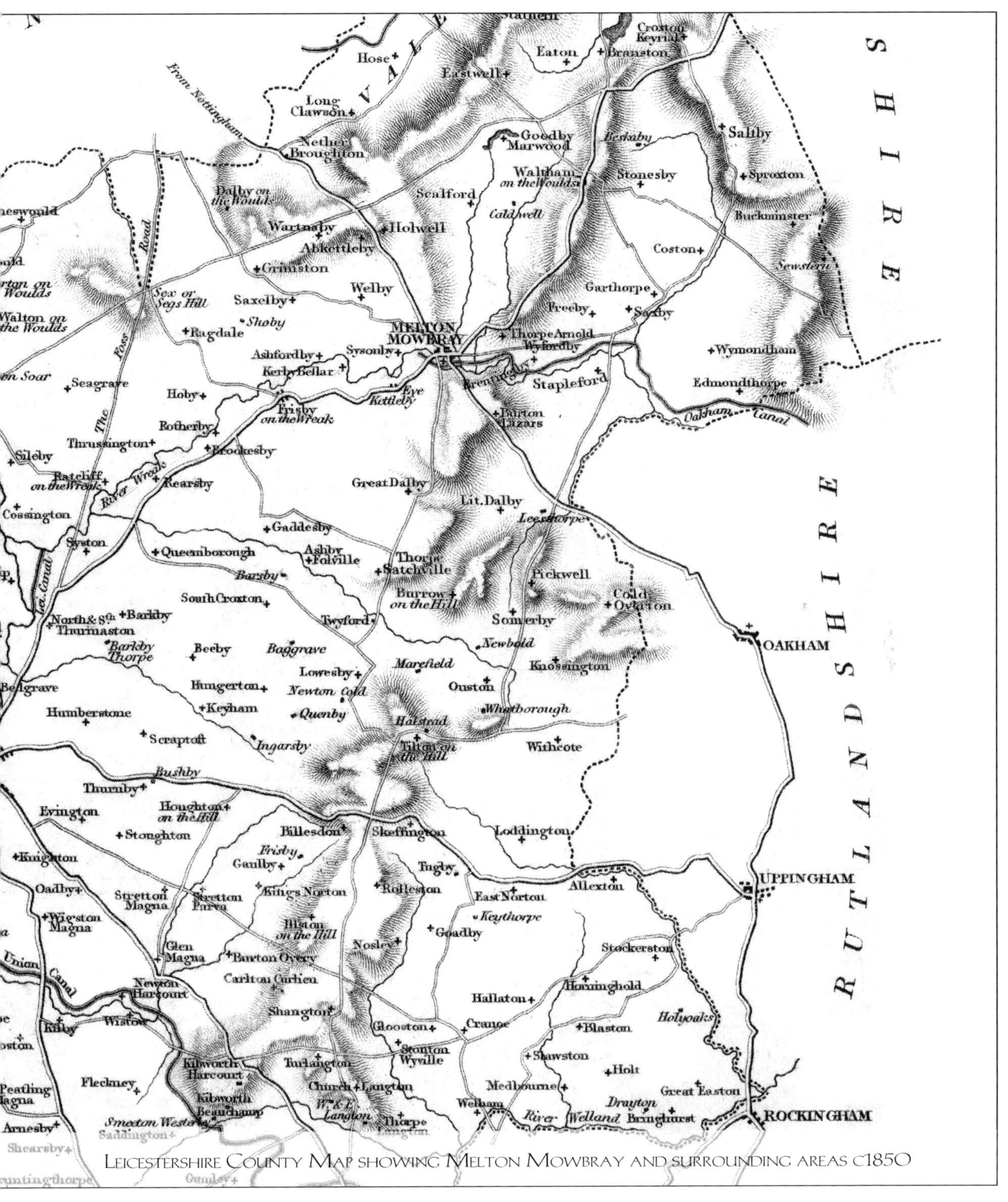

LEICESTER ROAD AND DALBY ROAD

THE BRIDGE AND THE CHURCH 1932 85170

LEICESTER ROAD AND DALBY ROAD

MAIN PICTURE: DALBY ROAD 1932 85175

RIGHT: LEICESTER ROAD C1950 M60007

On the left of the photograph is Egerton Lodge and the Memorial Gardens. The pedestrians are crossing the Lady Wilton Bridge, which spans the River Eye.

FAR RIGHT: THE WAR MEMORIAL HOSPITAL C1955 M60030

Colonel Charles Wyndham built Wyndham Lodge, on Ankle Hill, in 1906. In 1920, Colonel Richard Dalgleish bought Wyndham Lodge and paid for it to be converted into a War Memorial Hospital. The hospital opened in 1922.

LEICESTER ROAD AND DALBY ROAD

The picturesque Lady Wilton Bridge (85170, page 54) was built in 1822 replacing an earlier bridge, situated about 100 yards to the west. The old bridge had seven arches, one of which was paid for by the Harborough family. A plaque commemorating this is built into the present bridge, and can be viewed from the Memorial Gardens.

Dalby Road (85175, left) which leads off Leicester Road, used to be home to a number of hunting lodges. Warwick Lodge, built in 1902, was the last of the large hunting boxes to be built in Melton. It was originally owned by the Duke of Hamilton called Hamilton Lodge. The Lodge's name was changed when the Countess of Warwick purchased it a few years later. Notable visitors included the Duke and Duchess of Gloucester, who rented the house in 1935 for the hunting season. In 1955 the Melton and Belvoir Rural District Council bought Warwick Lodge to use as their offices and Council Chamber.

EGERTON LODGE

Egerton Lodge is an impressive house on the banks of the River Eye. It is very close to the town centre, standing at the junction of the High Street and Leicester Road (M60161, page 60). In the 1820s the 2nd Earl of Wilton bought the Lodge and the surrounding lands. The Earl soon began making extensive alterations and additions, rebuilding much of the house and outbuildings. He employed the skills of the Wyatt family, the famous architects, who were responsible for much of the work at Royal Windsor.

Egerton Lodge soon became the heart of the Melton Mowbray hunting scene. It was very popular amongst the neighbouring nobility and to dine at Egerton Lodge was to be accepted into Melton's highest circles. Egerton Lodge attracted many famous visitors. In the mid 1800s the Duke of Wellington, and also the former Prime Minister, Disraeli, stayed here. And in 1873 the Earl and Countess received their most esteemed visitor; the Prince of Wales, who was to become King Edward VII. A grand ball was held in his honour.

The Earl and Countess were also prominent amongst the wider community in Melton; they helped with local fund raising events, and the Earl attended town meetings. The Earl was known as a colourful character and an excellent huntsman. He died at Egerton Lodge in 1882 and as a mark of respect, all the town's shops and businesses closed on the day of his funeral.

In 1928 the heirs to Egerton Lodge put it up for auction but failed to find a buyer for the entire estate. Egerton Lodge, which had been the social centre for Melton's high society for nearly a century, was now to be divided. The Urban District Council bought Egerton Lodge in 1928. They used the house as their offices for nearly 40 years. Today the Lodge is a home for the elderly.

The Town Estate acquired the ornamental gardens at the front of the house. This provided an ideal opportunity for the Melton branch of the British Legion site for a memorial to those who had died in the First World War. They wanted to replace the existing wooden memorial, close to the bandstand in the Town Park, which had begun to decay. The Town Estate agreed to turn the gardens at Egerton Lodge into Memorial Gardens. They have continued to maintain the uniquely-shaped yew trees and the Victorian shrubbery. The terrace of the house is now a memorial to those Meltonians who were lost in the World Wars.

EGERTON LODGE C1950 M60018

The grand house, with its bay and sash windows, is typical of the Georgian style.

The Urban District Council also bought the gardens to the north of the Lodge. This was partly used for a car park and a college. It was also used to build a by-pass between the High Street and Nottingham Road, to relieve the congested Nottingham Street. The oldest part of the house, dating from the 18th century, had to be demolished to make way for the new road,

EGERTON LODGE

Wilton Road, pictured in M60161, page 60, to the right of the T-junction. Wilton Road also provides better access to the Lady Wilton Bridge and Leicester Road, which continues to the left of the photograph.

The gardens contain some unique relics of the past. Close to the bridge, built into the wall of the gardens, is a medieval archway. This originally formed the front door of the Manor of St John of Jerusalem, in Nottingham Street. It dates from the 14th century and was relocated to the War Memorial Gardens in 1961. Nearer the house is the Bread Door. This wooden door originally came from The Limes in Sherrard Street; it contains a hatch through which bread was passed to the poor.

EGERTON LODGE

Two visitors enjoy a walk in the
Memorial Gardens. Behind them
is the River Eye, and the Lady
Wilton Bridge on Leicester Road.

EGERTON LODGE

EGERTON LODGE GARDENS 1932 85174

This photograph, and 85171, pages 62-63
show views of the lodge from the banks of the
Eye, with groups enjoying the gardens.
On the opposite side of the river, the side from
where the photographs were taken, is Egerton
Park, also owned by the Town Estate. It is still
used today as cricket grounds.

EGERTON LODGE

Egerton Lodge 1932 85171

ST MARY'S CHURCH

ST MARY'S CHURCH 1927 80308

St Mary's 100ft-high tower dominates the town. The clerestory can be clearly seen along the length of the nave and transept. The clerestory and the top section of the tower were added around 1500.

ST MARY'S CHURCH

The beautiful church of St Mary the Virgin is the largest and arguably the most impressive parish church in Leicestershire.

The oldest part of the church is the lower section of the tower. This is thought to date from the 12th century and is likely to have formed part of an earlier building. The majority of the church is in the decorated style and dates from the late 13th and early 14th centuries. St Mary's is built in a cruciform shape. The transepts on either side of the nave are particularly remarkable. St Mary's is one of only five churches in England with aisled transepts which are

ST MARY'S CHURCH

St Mary's Church, the Interior 1927 80311

usually only seen in cathedrals. Most of the statues on the exterior of the church were lost after the Reformation. The only remaining statue is a 600-year-old figure of St Peter holding a key, which stands over the north door.

Inside, the church is excellently lit because of the rows of clear clerestory windows that run above the nave and transepts. Over the central arch is a royal coat of arms of King Charles II, dated 1682. However, it has been discovered that it actually dates from 1632: the reign of Charles I. Small holes were found in this plaque, and it is thought that it was used by the Parliamentarians during the civil war for target practice.

Lying in a recess of the south wall is the figure of a crusader. The inscription on the figure dates it to 1150, although evidence suggests that 1303 is a more likely date. There are also indications that several altars for chantry chapels previously existed in the transepts. On the east aisle of the south transept there are a number of tombs and monuments. One raised tomb is that of Edward and Katherine Pate, who died in the 1590s. Their life-size figures are represented in Elizabethan dress and lie side by side. Another tomb is that of a lady of the Burgeis family. The woman is shown in 14th-century dress and is exceptionally well preserved.

Photograph 80313, page 69 shows the north transept of the church, looking through to the south transept. The brass chandelier pictured here hangs in the centre of the transept and there is another in the centre of the south transept. The chandeliers were originally hung in the nave in 1746. The organ on the left was built in 1955 but incorporates some of the pipes from the earlier organ of 1897. From 1914 to 1924, St Mary's was home to the famous organist and choirmaster Sir Malcolm Sargent.

A spiral staircase leads up the tower. The belfry contains 10 bells, one of which is thought to date from the 14th century, making it one of the oldest in use in England. There is also a small sanctus bell dating from the end of the 17th century. Other precious relics include a 16th-century brass, which is a memorial to Cristofer Gonson and his wife, and a Tudor cupboard in the vestry, which is still in use today.

The grand Galilee porch (M60002, page 69) is typical of the Decorated period. Although eroded, the ball-flower ornament around the windows and door can be clearly seen.

In Georgian times, the porch housed the town fire engine, which is now in the Carnegie museum. During the early 19th century, the graveyard in front of the church became unacceptably over-crowded. In 1845, after many complaints, a new cemetery was opened on St Mary's Way.

ST MARY'S CHURCH

ST MARY'S CHURCH

The font was installed in 1847 and has a beautifully carved wooden cover. Until 1930, the font stood in what is now the clergy vestry. The window behind the font is largely made up of medieval stained glass that was collected from St Mary's, other churches in the area and the Bede House. It was pieced together early in the 19th century. Most of the other stained glass windows in the church are Victorian.

RIGHT:
ST MARY'S CHURCH, NORTH TRANSEPT 1927 80313

BELOW:
THE GALILEE PORCH C1950 M60002

OTHER CHURCHES IN MELTON MOWBRAY

ABOVE:
THE WELBY LANE MISSION C1955 M60044

RIGHT:
ST JOHN THE BAPTIST CATHOLIC CHURCH C1955
M60038

This church was built in 1842 in the Italian style made popular by the celebrated architect, Pugin. Stained glass in the east window depicts the church's main benefactors kneeling at Christ's feet.

FAR RIGHT:
THE BAPTIST CHURCH C1955 M60043

The Baptist Church was built in 1872 near the site of the Sheep Cross. The £2200 cost was raised by subscription. It originally seated a congregation of 400. The building was recently considerably renovated and is now owned by the Christian group, Covenant Life Melton.

OTHER CHURCHES IN MELTON MOWBRAY

ABOVE: SYSONBY CHURCH c1955
M60062

Sysonby church is one of Melton's four Church of
England churches.

LEFT: THE CONGREGATIONAL CHURCH
c1955 M60045

Before the building of this church in 1822, the
Congregationalists of Melton gathered in the
old Playhouse on the High Street. Also known
as the Independents, the Congregationalists
were important in the opposition to Charles I
during the Civil War. The Congregationalists
and Presbyterians joined forces in 1972, and the
church is now the United Reformed Church.

MELTON MOWBRAY

OTHER CHURCHES IN MELTON MOWBRAY

RIGHT:
SAGE CROSS METHODIST CHURCH
C1955 M60021

The first Methodist church in Melton was built in 1796 at a time when Melton's Wesleyan Society had only eleven members. A new church was built on the site in 1808, and enlarged in 1825, when Melton's Methodist population reached one hundred. The church was again rebuilt in 1871 to seat 700.

BELOW:
SHERRARD STREET METHODIST CHURCH C1955 M60019

The Primitive Methodists of Melton built their first chapel in Goodriche Street in 1845. The Sherrard Street Methodist Church, built in 1888, was demolished in 1973 when the Methodist churches regrouped.

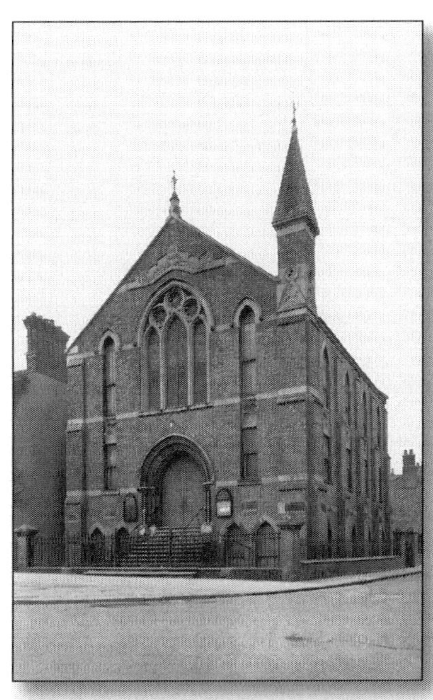

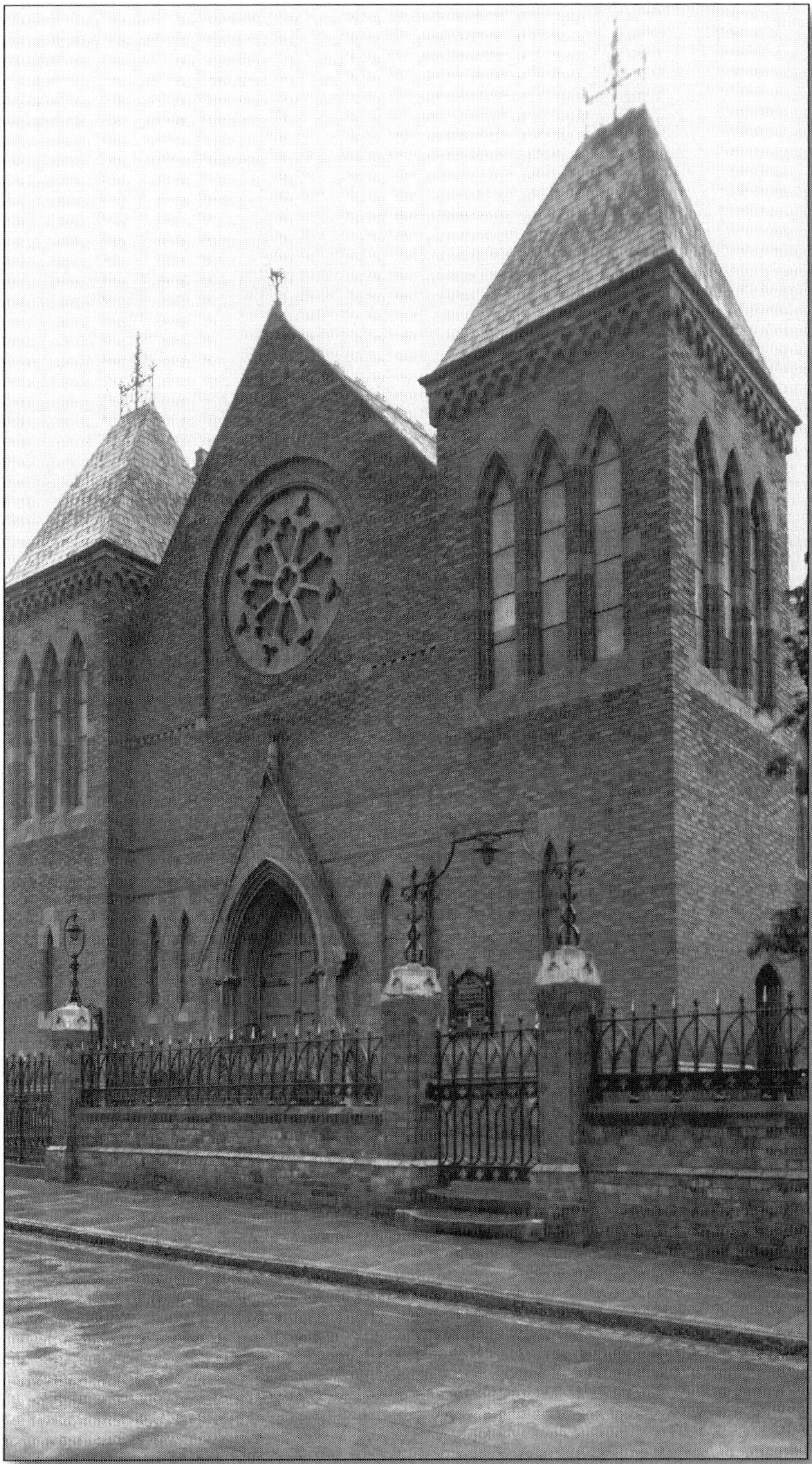

MELTON'S SCHOOLS

Melton Mowbray has a long history of providing education for children of the parish; it is even believed that a school existed here as early as 1347. Free education became a legal requirement in the Education Act of 1850, by which time Melton had been providing free schools for over 300 years. These free schools were only possible because of the Town Estate. From 1577 it was agreed that the Town Estate would be responsible for funding the boys' Grammar School, which was located in Spital End (now Nottingham Street), probably opposite the former Corn Exchange.

A Town Meeting of 1793 proved beyond any doubt that Melton was ahead of the times in terms of education, by deciding that a girls' school should be opened. The Town Estate records state 'that 60 girls be admitted to the school to be taught reading, knitting, plain work, writing and accounts'. The school was to cater for girls aged between seven and twelve years old. Now Melton could boast of providing free education for any child, regardless of their wealth, sex or social background. The girls' school was built in King Street and in 1818 a new boys' school was opened on the same site. The old site in Nottingham Street had been too small to cope with the rising population in the town.

In 1849 controversy arose concerning religious education in the King Street school. At that time many Meltonians were dissenters or non-conformists, and they were concerned that the school was trying to indoctrinate their children. The school was supposedly non-denominational, yet the staff were all Anglican. A Town Meeting was called, chaired by the Earl of Wilton, and it was decided that the school should be split in two; 286 parents wished their children to go to a church school and 196 wanted their children to attend a British or non-denominational school. The building was divided in two, and two separate committees were appointed to manage the schools. The funding from the Town Estate was now shared between the two schools.

During the following years both the Church School and the British School suffered from overcrowding. In 1853, in order to relieve pressure on the King Street schools, a Church of England Infants School was built on Norman Street. In 1889 an extension to the British School was also built, to the rear of the King Street site.

Towards the end of the 19th century the financial burden of

the schools on the Town Estate was considerable. New national standards and the increasing population meant that the Town Estate could no longer meet the costs of maintaining the schools. In the early 20th century the Town Estate handed over control of the schools to the Local Education Authority under the County Council. However, to this day the Town Estate donates additional funds to Melton's schools. Today Melton continues to provide local children with excellent educational facilities. There are numerous primary and secondary schools as well as special schools and colleges of higher education.

THE GRAMMAR SCHOOL C1955 M60022

The Grammar School, now named King Edward VII School, was founded by the County Council in 1910. In the 1960s it ceased to be a grammar school, and today it is open to all children from 14-18. In 1977 the school was awarded Technology status, and it is now recognised as one of the country's leading colleges in its field.

SARSON SCHOOL C1960 M60127

The neighbouring Sarson High School was opened in 1952 and caters for 11-14 year olds. In 1999 it merged with King Edward VII School. Despite the merger it retains much of its independence and is known as The Sarson Centre. King Edward VII School now caters for the full secondary age range. Both the schools are situated on an extensive green field site off Burton Road, overlooking Melton Mowbray.

Fernley High School c1965 M60186

Fernley High School was founded in 1964.

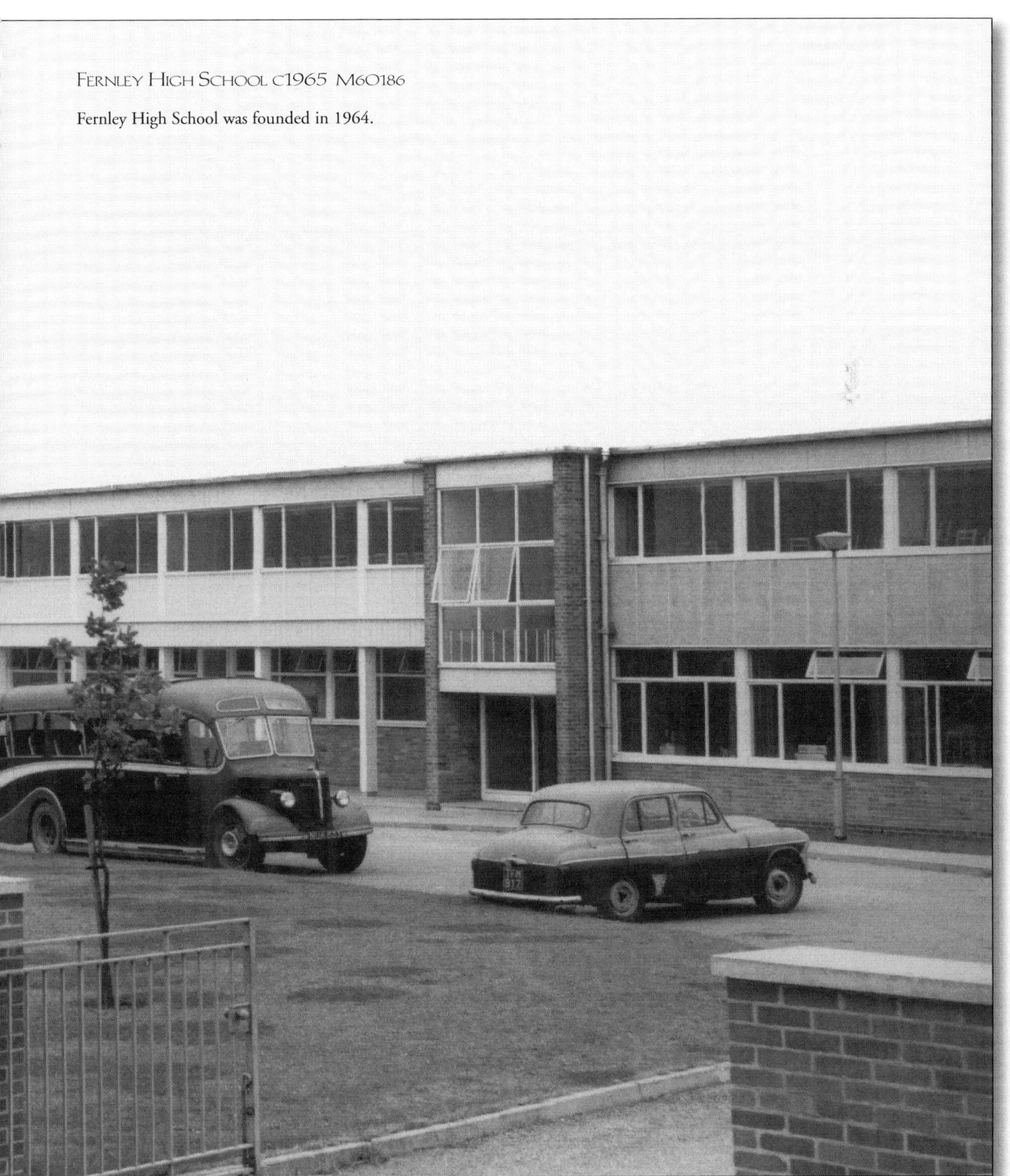

THE TOWN PARKS

E xtensive and tranquil parks can be found at the very heart of Melton Mowbray. They are a welcome haven from the busy roads and shopping streets of the town centre. Once again Melton has the Town Estate to thank for providing these parks. However, they were not always as peaceful as they are today; the Town Estate acquired its first parkland after the Play Close riots of 1848.

The Play Close (M60150, page 80) is an area of the park bordered by St Mary's church and Park Lane. For many years before the riots, local people had used the land for recreational purposes and town fairs. However, in the 1840s a number of businesses on Park Lane began to encroach upon the land, building outhouses, fences and even pig sties. This caused increasing resentment in the town and a group of young men called the 'Young Nationals' decided to take matters into their own hands. They tore down fences and demolished many of the buildings on the encroached land. The riot ended when Special Constables apprehended several of the men, many of whom were later fined.

However, the problem of encroachment remained unresolved and there was still unrest in the town. The Feoffees (those responsible for the land owned by the Town Estate) decided to send a delegation to Lord Melbourne in London, the lord of the manor, who owned the Play Close. He eventually agreed to sell the land to the Town Estate, along with the rights to the market. The Play Close was then secured for use by the townspeople. Today the Play Close is incorporated into the large Town Park and still hosts the Melton Show, which is held annually on the Bank Holiday Monday at the end of May.

In 1908 the Town Estate bought a new section of land in Leicester Street, which enabled them to greatly improve the accessibility to the Town Park and the Play Close. The entrance was rebuilt with impressive new cast iron gates. In the late 1980s the park was enlarged once more, with the addition of picturesque Priors Close with its winding paths, trees, small lakes and rustic bridge (M60009, page 81). This land was developed by one of Melton's major employers, Pedigree Petfoods, to commemorate its 50th year in the town.

By the River c1950 M60008

Young boys play on the banks of the River Eye. The river is also a popular spot for ducks and swans.

THE TOWN PARKS

Right: The Park c1965 M60150

This is the area known as the Play Close with St Mary's church in the background. There is still a children's play area on this site. Dogs and children can be seen playing in the paddling pool in the foreground of the photograph. The pool was built in 1934, and was very popular until the nearby swimming baths were opened. Unfortunately, in 1986 the pool had to be filled in due to vandalism.

Below Left: The Bandstand c1955 M60025

The bandstand was built during the improvements to the park in the early 1900s. It is now a Grade 2 listed building and concerts are performed here every Sunday between May and September.

Below Right: The Rustic Bridge c1950 M60009

An unusual reminder of by-gone days are the tops of the lock gates from the old canal which are hidden amongst the trees in the park. The Melton canal which opened in 1794, ran through the land that is now the park. The canal closed in the 19th century after the opening of the railways.

THE TOWN PARKS

SPORTING FACILITIES

SPORTING FACILITIES

The Town Estate also provides Melton with excellent sporting facilities. In 1919 it purchased the land alongside Leicester Road, across the river from the Play Close. Leicester Road Sports Ground was developed and now contains putting and bowling greens. There are also tennis courts which can be covered by an inflatable airdome, allowing people to play tennis regardless of weather conditions.

In the 1930s the Town Estate bought Egerton Park, a large field on the opposite side of Leicester Road. The land soon became the town's main cricket ground and it is let to the Egerton Park Cricket Club. The Town Estate also owns the Asfordby Road Sports Ground which contains a 9-hole golf course. The All England Ground on Saxby Road which the Town Estate lets to local clubs, provides facilities for cricket, rugby and football.

TOP: THE BOWLING GREEN C1965 M60152

This is the Leicester Road Bowling Green which has been home to the Park Bowls Club for many years.

BOTTOM: THE SWIMMING BATHS C1965 M60154

In 1941 the Town Estate acquired land between Leicester Road and Dalby Road. The Waterfield Swimming Baths were built on this site in 1965 and they are still popular today. Young boys are fishing on the River Eye in front of the baths.

Ordnance Survey Map

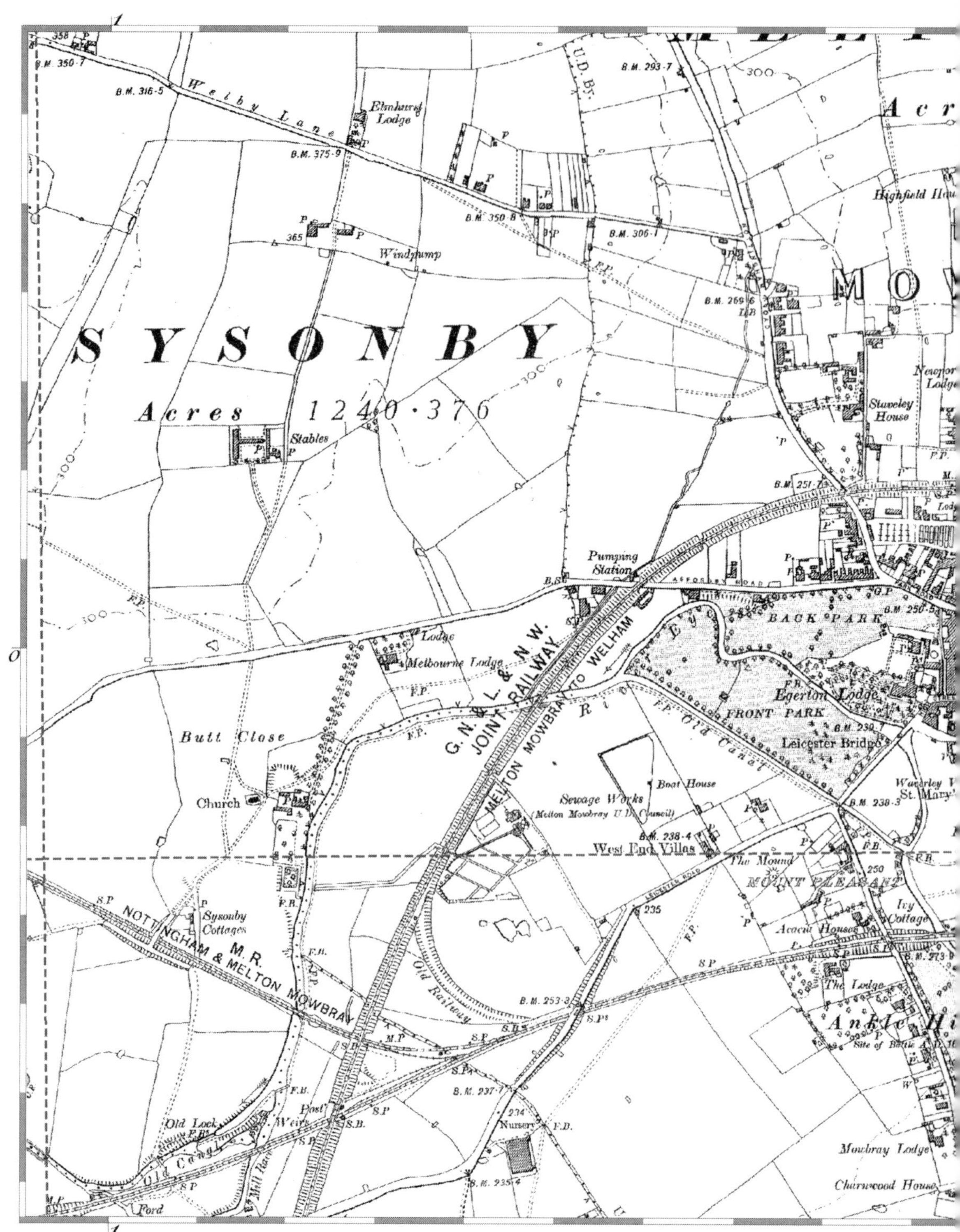

Ordnance Survey Map

Ordnance Survey Map showing Melton Mowbray and surrounding areas 1884–1902

NAMES OF PRE-PUBLICATION BUYERS

The following people have kindly supported this book by purchasing limited edition copies prior to publication.

Mr G R Ainge & Mrs J M Ainge, Melton Mowbray

In memory of Charlie Aley

The Aley Family, Melton Mowbray

In loving memory of Annie Anderson

To Andrew from Mum & Dad, Melton Mowbray

Pam Ashby

Mrs P F Ball

To Richard Batsford on your Retirement

To our sons, love Mummy & Daddy Bird

Sue Bower, Melton Mowbray

Mrs C Bowes & Miss S Bowes, Melton Mowbray

Jason Campden

The Cockayne Family, Melton Mowbray

Andrew W M Cooper, Melton Mowbray

N Crow

Gerald F Culley, Melton Mowbray

Paul Curtis

Judith Dalton (nee Brotherhood)

Tom & Gloria Dickinson, Melton Mowbray

Peter Joel Ecob, Melton Mowbray

Paul Eggleton

The Forks Family, Melton Mowbray

Lauren V Freeman, Melton Mowbray

Adrian Arthur Gilson, Melton Mowbray

Andrew Walter Green, Melton Mowbray 2005

Trevor & Janice Harbin, Asfordby

In memory of Tom & Freda Hood of Melton

Keith & Jo Hunter, Melton Mowbray

Stuart would like to say Jayne,
    Thank you, I love you

Malcolm Johnson, Melton Mowbray

Mr C Jones, Melton Mowbray

S H Kendall, Melton Mowbray

Ian Kent, 50 years in Melton Mowbray

Gillian Lane, Thorpe Arnold

The Lawrie Family, Melton Mowbray

Peter W Marsh, Somerby, Melton Mowbray

For my daughter, Zoe Elysia Morgan

For my daughter, Danielle Anne Morgan

Mrs Pauline North and the late Cecil North

Mr R M & Mrs E C Padgett, Melton Mowbray

Michael Peters, Asfordby, Melton Mowbray

Mr J & Mrs J Powroznik, Melton Mowbray

To Ian Pritchett, World's Greatest Dad xxx

In memory of Granny & Grandad Radford

Mr Albert Rutledge & Mrs Millie Rutledge

Doris, Arthur, Graham, Beverly & Marie Sisson

To my loving husband, Robert Kingsley Smith,
    love Moira

Barbara Todd, Melton Mowbray

In loving remembrance of the Twins

For my parents Ron & Barbara Wallbanks

In loving memory of Mr Cecil Whitfield

FRANCIS FRITH'S
TOWN&CITY
MEMORIES

FRITH PRODUCTS & SERVICES

Francis Frith would doubtless be pleased to know that the pioneering publishing venture he started in 1860 still continues today. Over a hundred and forty years later, The Francis Frith Collection continues in the same innovative tradition and is now one of the foremost publishers of vintage photographs in the world. Some of the current activities include:

INTERIOR DECORATION

Today Frith's photographs can be seen framed and as giant wall murals in thousands of pubs, restaurants, hotels, banks, retail stores and other public buildings throughout the country. In every case they enhance the unique local atmosphere of the places they depict and provide reminders of gentler days in an increasingly busy and frenetic world.

PRODUCT PROMOTIONS

Frith products are used by many major companies to promote the sales of their own products or to reinforce their own history and heritage. Frith promotions have been used by Hovis bread, Courage beers, Scots Porage Oats, Colman's mustard, Cadbury's foods, Mellow Birds coffee, Dunhill pipe tobacco, Guinness, and Bulmer's Cider.

GENEALOGY AND FAMILY HISTORY

As the interest in family history and roots grows world-wide, more and more people are turning to Frith's photographs of Great Britain for images of the towns, villages and streets where their ancestors lived; and, of course, photographs of the churches and chapels where their ancestors were christened, married and buried are an essential part of every genealogy tree and family album.

FRITH PRODUCTS

All Frith photographs are available Framed or just as Mounted Prints and Posters (size 23 x 16 inches). These may be ordered from the address below. Other products available are- Address Books, Calendars, Jigsaws, Canvas Prints, Coasters, Notelets and local and prestige books.

THE INTERNET

Already ninety thousand Frith photographs can be viewed and purchased on the internet through the Frith websites and a myriad of partner sites.

For more detailed information on Frith companies and products, look at this site:
www.francisfrith.com

See the complete list of Frith Books at: www.francisfrith.com
This web site is regularly updated with the latest list of publications from The Francis Frith Collection. If you wish to buy books relating to another part of the country that your local bookshop does not stock, you may purchase on-line.

For further information, trade, or author enquiries please contact us at the address below:
The Francis Frith Collection, Frith's Barn, Teffont, Salisbury, Wiltshire, England SP3 5QP.
Tel: +44 (0)1722 716 376 Fax: +44 (0)1722 716 881 Email: sales@francisfrith.co.uk

---

See Frith products on the internet at www.francisfrith.com